Liu Bolin : Hiding in the City

Essay by Geneviève Brisac All images selected from Liu Bolin's work

The incertitude principle and the gene of unreality

Geneviève Brisac

In 1970 I got my first camera. Around the same time, on the other side of the planet, the photographer Liu Bolin was being born.

I remember my camera very well. It was an Instamatic and I immediately fell in love with its shape, – light and rectangular – and its washing-machine-like name.

Photography seemed to me to be the supreme art, a fascinating activity combining the quest for beauty and for truth, the art of the painter, the journalist and the detective.

It was especially a good excuse to wander, knock at doors, and force people to stop in order to be fixed for all eternity on my black and yellow Kodak film.

I went on expeditions in the city. I photographed branches shaken by the wind, and walls scribbled over with inscriptions. I photographed the iron fencing surrounding a park, already red with autumn, old people sitting on a bench, and students smoking on the steps of the Pantheon. I snapped children building a shapeless castle on a pile of sand and birds on the edge of a brown puddle. I caught lovers by surprise, and I reenacted my favourite movie, Blow-Up by Antonioni, which I had seen not long beforehand.

While on the other side of the world, the great Cultural Revolution wrought its havoc, I was trying to capture the nature of things, the motion of my life.

Then suddenly I was seized by doubt: I would never be able to squeeze all of reality into my Instamatic's box. The world was escaping me. What was the point?

I became melancholic. The camera was like a Geiger counter, a measuring instrument made to assess something unknown, and I didn't know how to use it.

What was I searching for? I would have been hard pressed to answer this question. Did I want to stop the flow of time? Account for it? Tell the story of my life? I think not.

I used the camera as a question mark, the punctum that Roland Barthes talks about, to capture something whose nature was unknown to me, something I was incapable of seeing. Blow-Up, yes, exactly.

I took my film to get it developed and I waited anxiously for the results.

Had I got a lucky catch? Had I put to paper something invisible to the naked eye? Had I, by accident, captured a bird taking flight, the weapon used to commit a crime, the moment preceding the lovers' kiss, a lost object?

I thought of photography as an investigation undertaken in the dark, the gathering of evidence for a trial whose motive was still unclear.

Then I changed my focus. I started taking self-portraits. Profile shots, back shots, mirror shots: ironic black rectangle, please tell me who I am. I made installations: Me on a chair. At the window.

Photography is a window, but looking out on what?

I took my film to be developed and I waited anxiously for the result. What terrible anguish. I very soon got tired of self-portraits.

I think of all this while admiring the camouflage of Liu Bolin, the chameleon-man. I think of this phrase by Henri Michaux: Men, look at yourself in the paper.

What do you see?

What we see is the wonderfully successful realization of the question that I had tried to address with my Instamatic and my clumsiness. There is the world, and then there is the human being. The human being is so fragile that a ghost would be more solid. This human being, which is gradually fading away.

Liu Bolin photographs brick walls with their inscriptions which I cannot read, painted palisades, wooden palisades, aluminum palisades, construction sites with their girders, giant billboards that embody our world of consumption and development, concrete sewer pipes, a pile of wood and a pile of coal, a garbage dump and a supermarket aisle. This is Beijing. The Forbidden City. The Great Wall of China, a forest of thin trees, a wall of yellow and red flowers, a load of flags.

In the same vein of questioning, he takes pictures of the seats at the Scala, of its magic stage, of a bridge in Venice, the Milan Dome.

In each scene, each tableau one could say, the question is asked: ecce homo, where can Man be? Hidden in the carpet, as Henry James says. Here the carpet is a palisade, a wall, a painted canvas, a façade, and so the man is hidden in the folds, in the colours; he is almost invisible – I was going to say invincible. It's metaphysical and childish at the same time.

One can distinguish the man each time: his feet stick out, or else it's his face, the contour of his transparent body creates a problem. The man is still there. Stubborn, always there, weak and upright, eyes closed.

I recognize in his prey-like immobility the questions which, with Instamatic in hand, I discovered at the very time when Liu was being born. What does seeing mean, and who am I? If I am seen, if I am discovered, what will happen? And where do I belong? Questions that are more political than they seem.

Liu Bolin is everywhere. I recognize him and I salute his shadow. Yes, I see his sober silhouette, his arms quietly laid out alongside his body, the way he holds his head – in all his works except one. This one time, I took much longer to find him, it took me more time to experience the childish pleasure, the real relief of one who has found a long-lost friend, the living presence – Liu Bolin – whom I knew to be hiding in his picture, like a child hiding in order to be found.

This one time, I didn't find him immediately.

I even made the absurd hypothesis that he wasn't there. Liu, are you there?

The monastery is graceful. I scan the statues, the paintings, the plants, the stones, ah! Phew! There's a foot sticking out, Liu is there. I tell myself that even the monastery was unable to absorb Liu.

Liu Bolin, firm and fragile, unassignable chameleon, photographer.

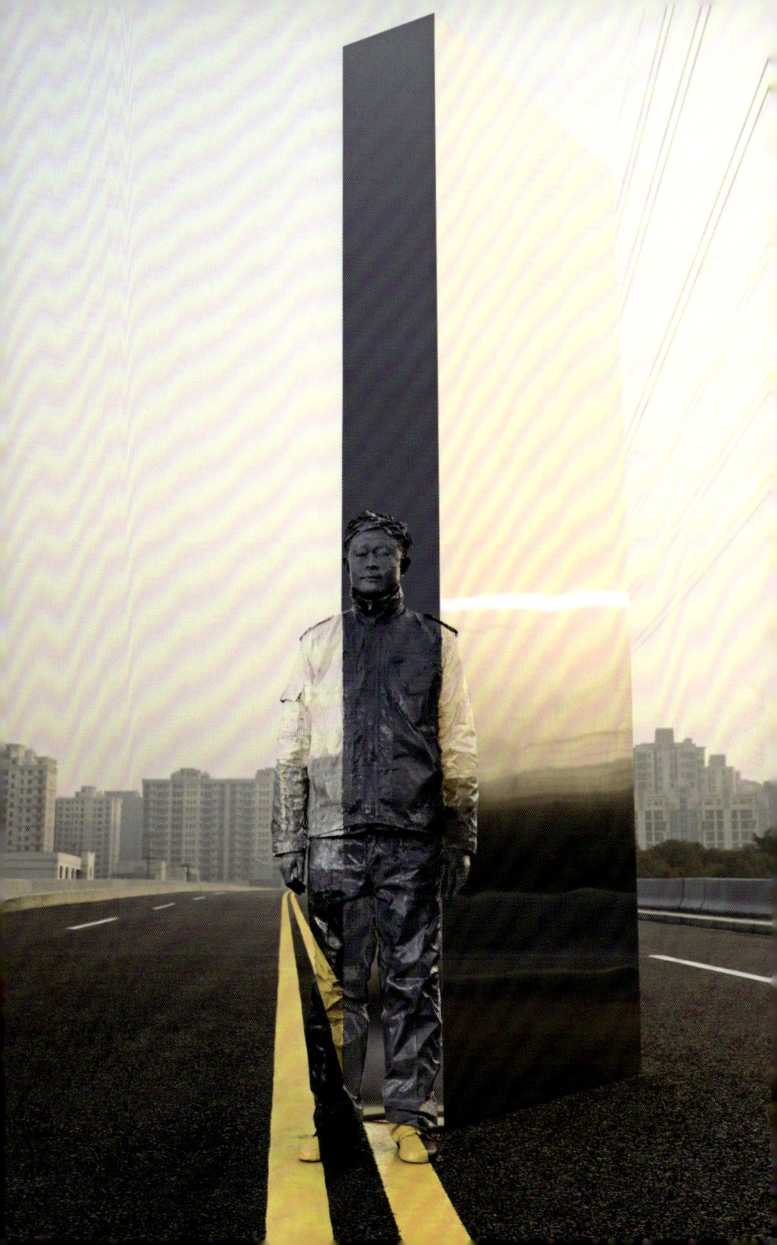

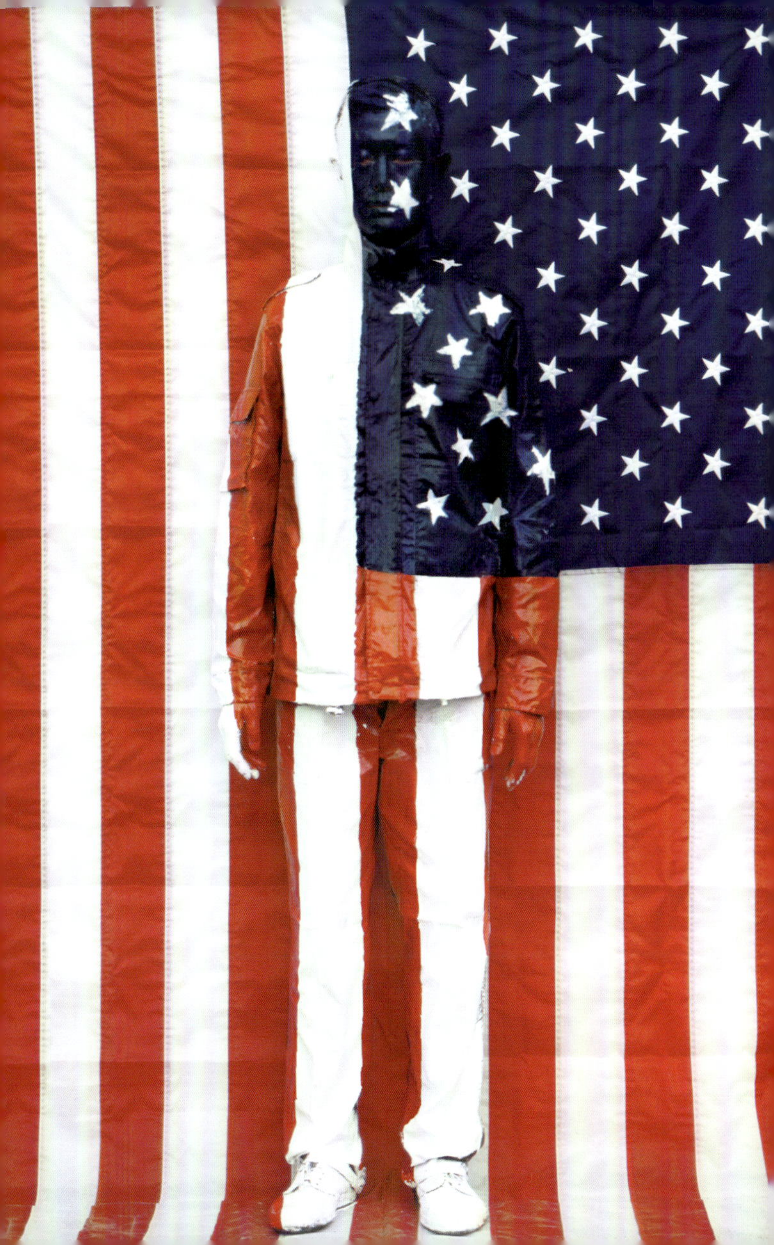

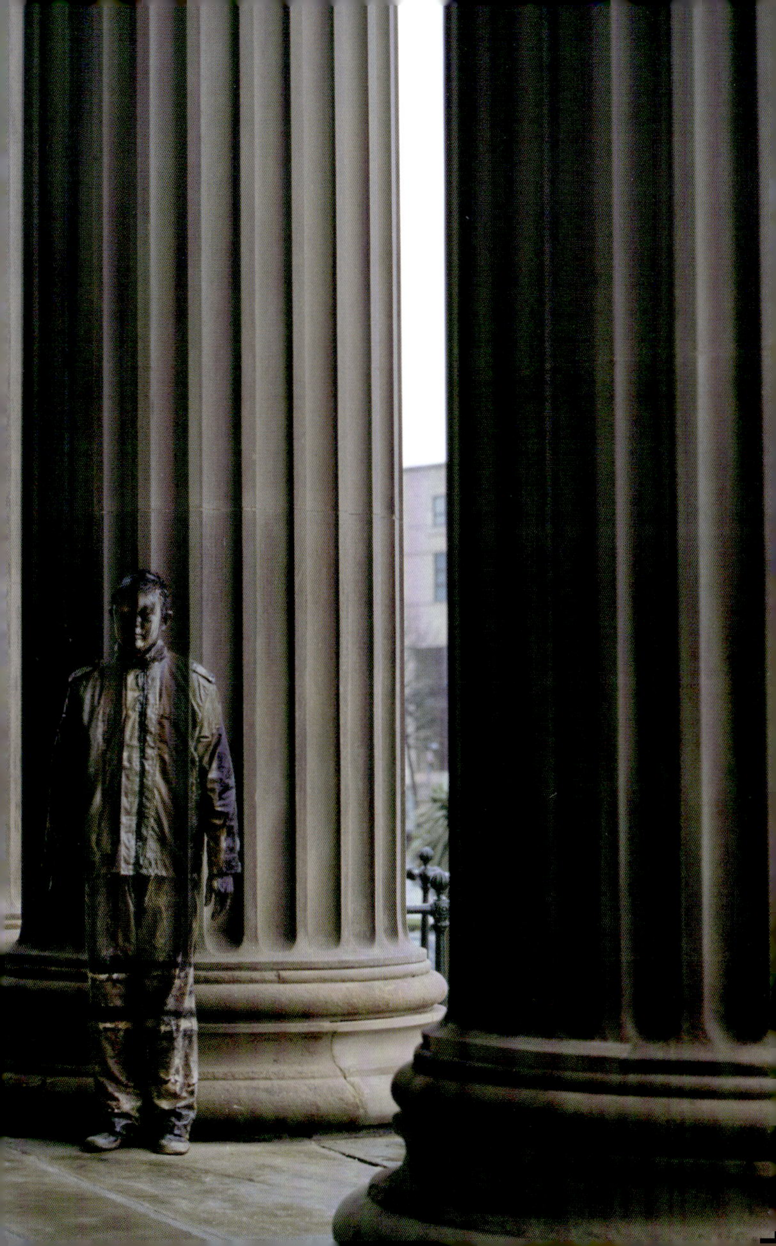

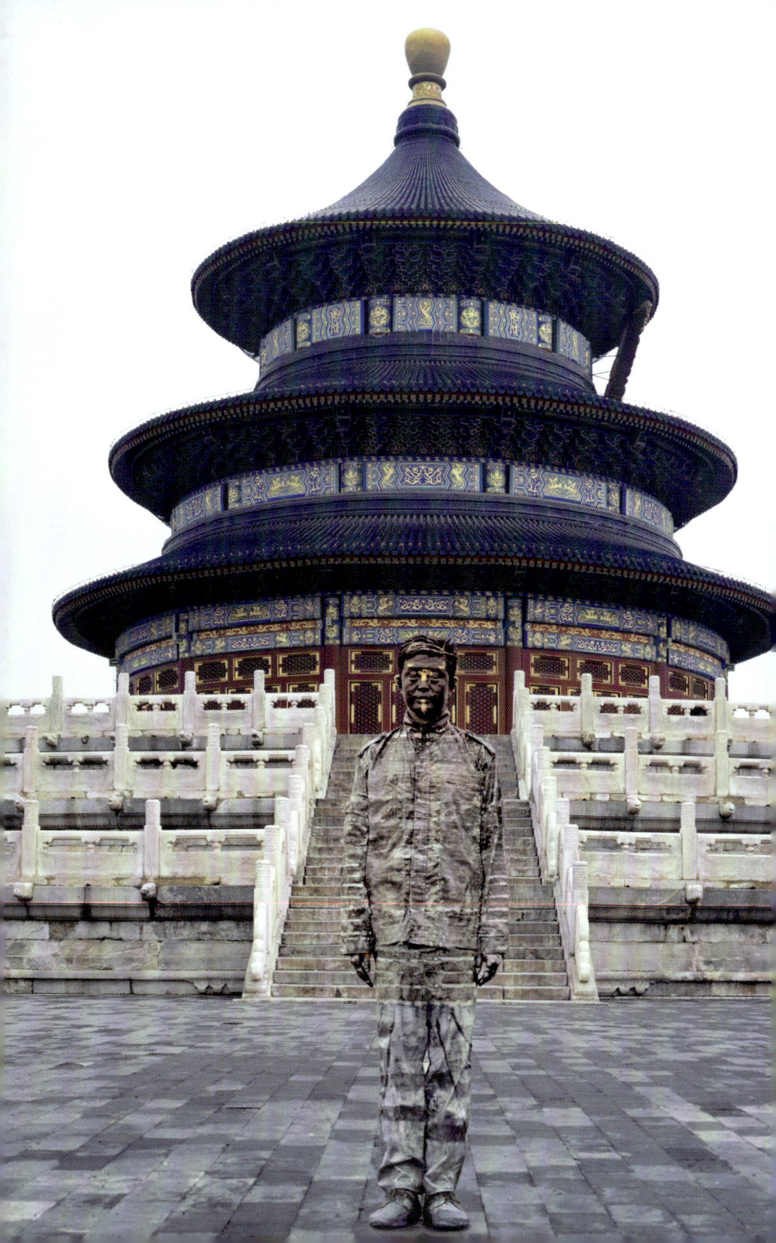

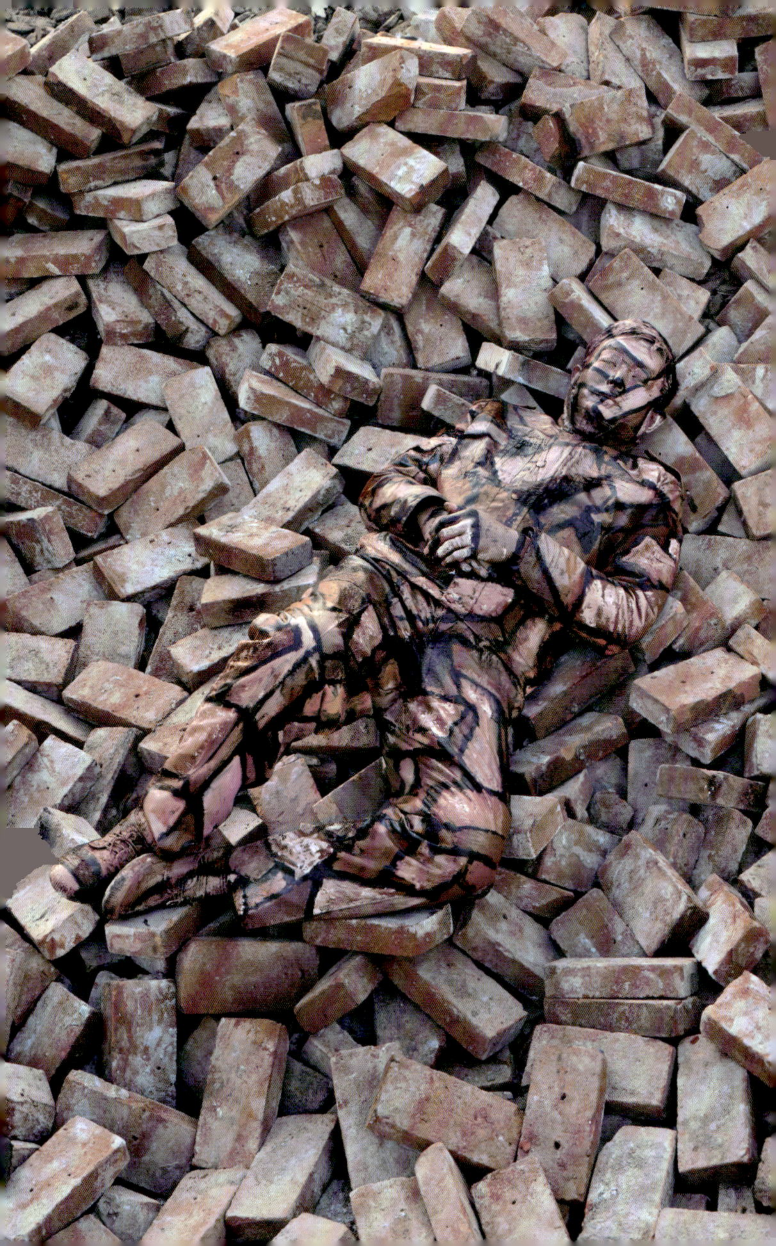

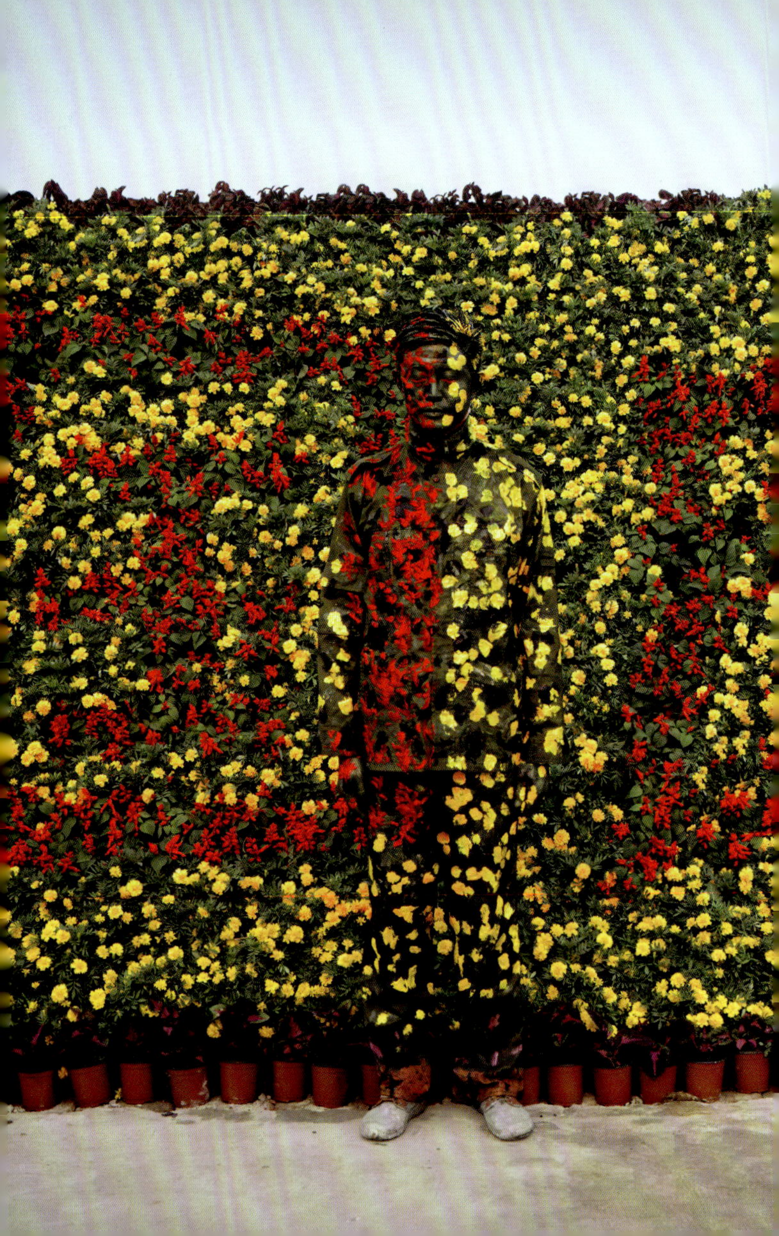

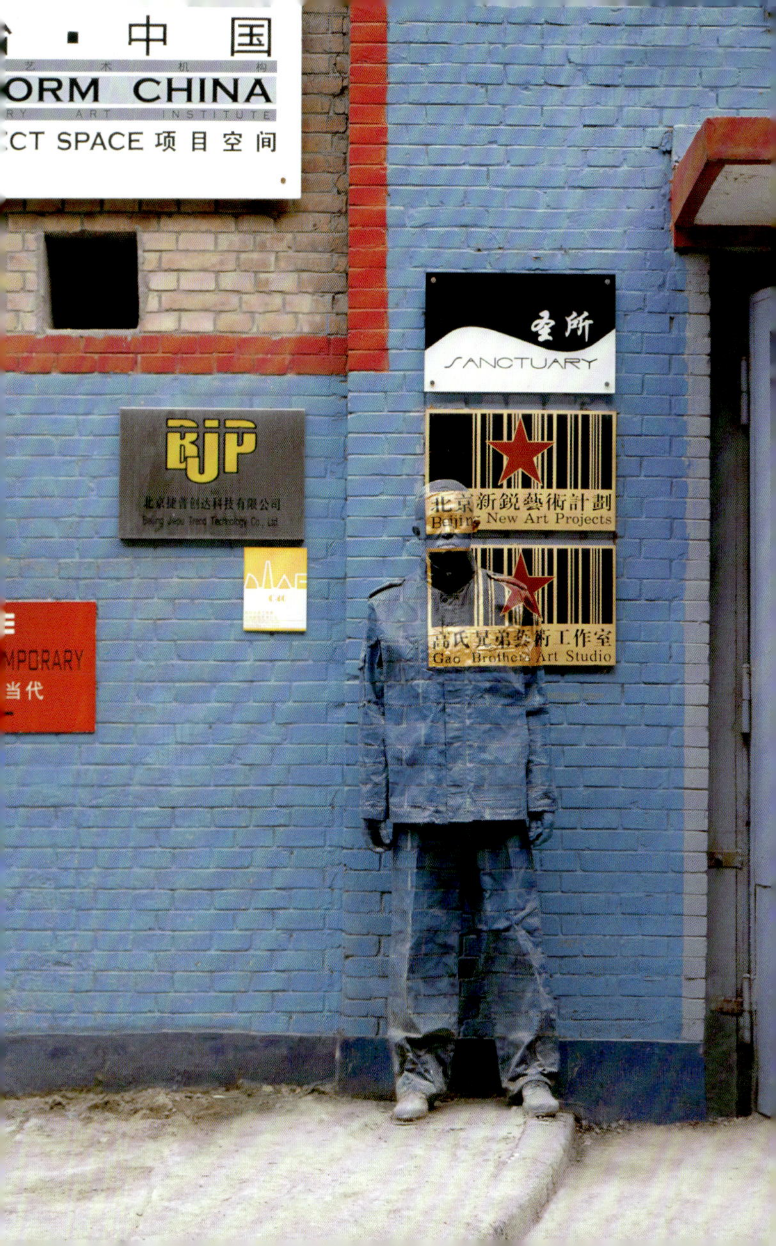

中 国
ORM CHINA
CT SPACE 项目空间
圣所
SANCTUARY
BJP
北京捷普创达科技有限公司
北京新銳藝術計劃
New Art Projects
高氏兄弟藝術工作室
Gao Brothers Art Studio
MPORARY
当代

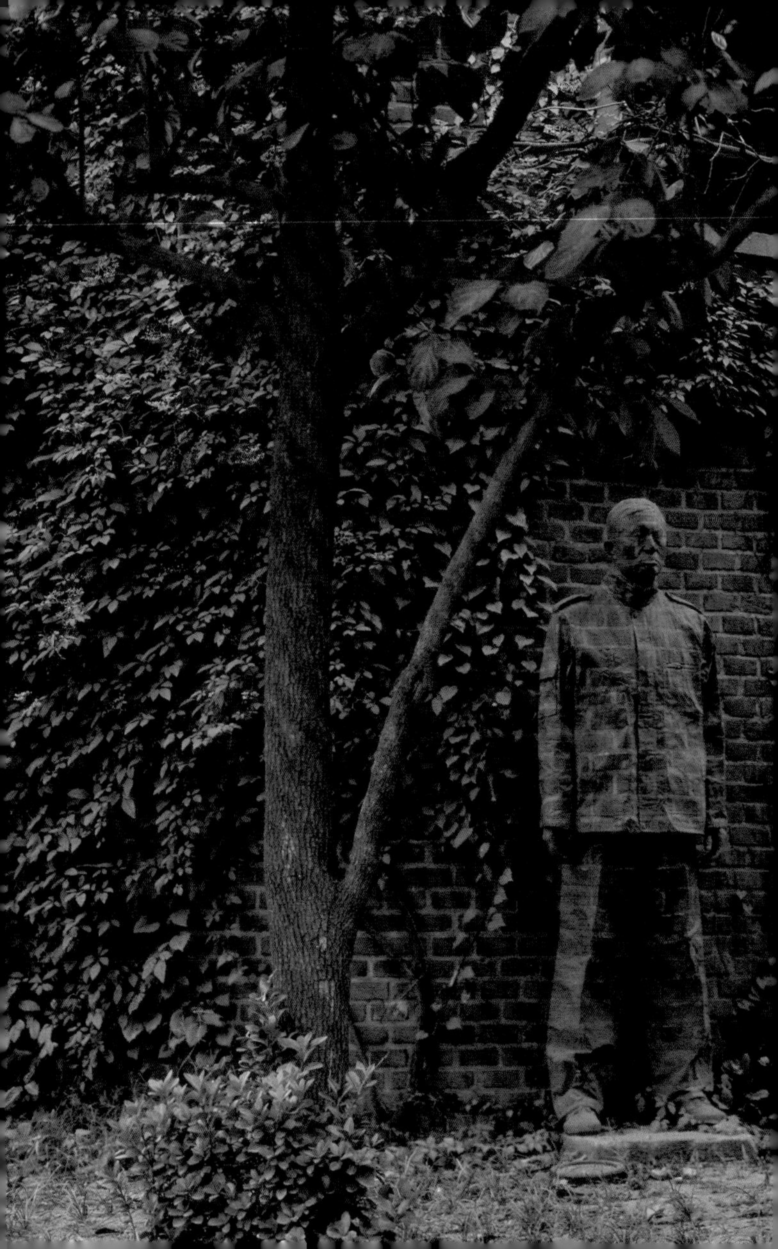

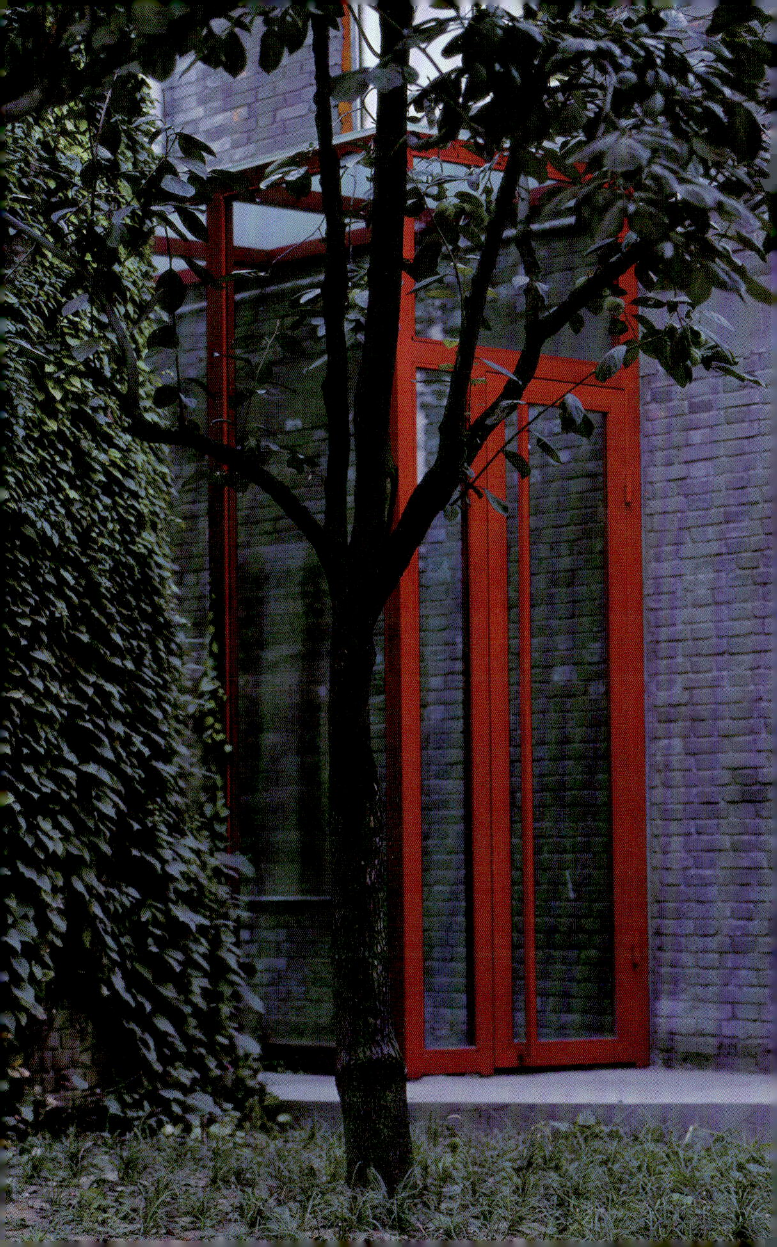

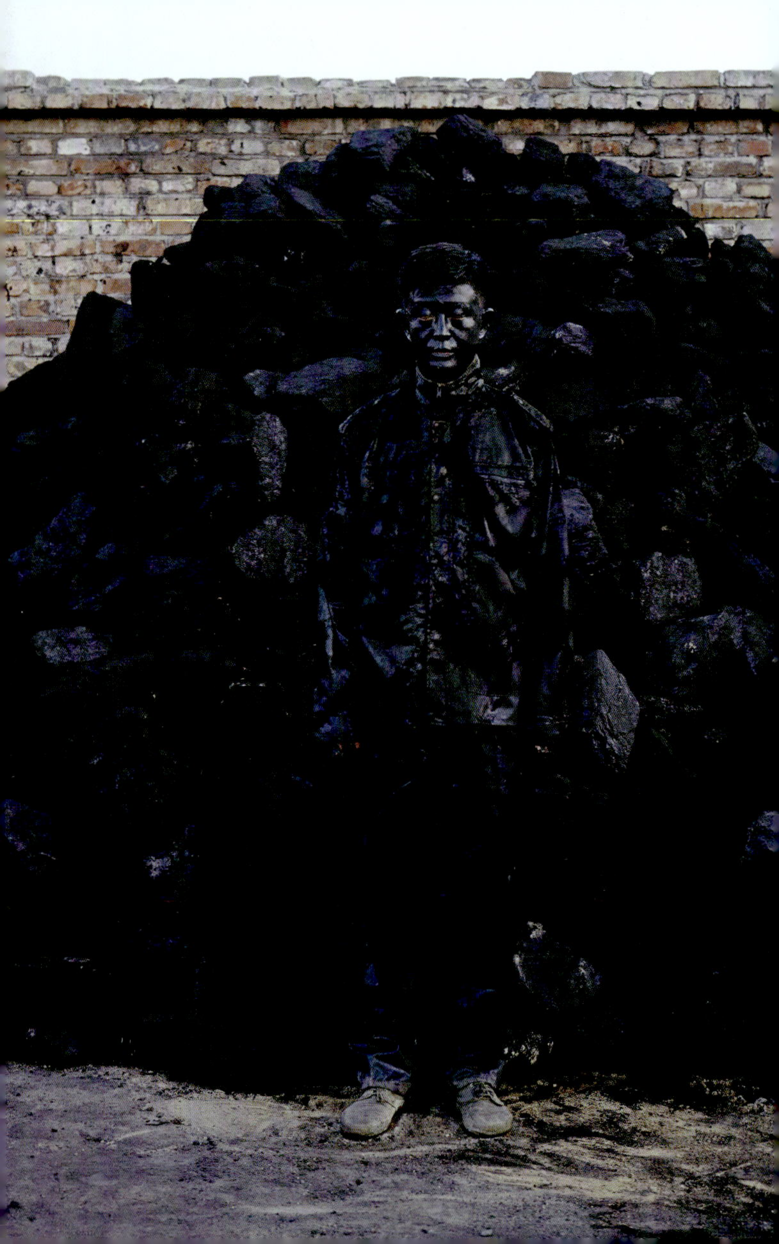

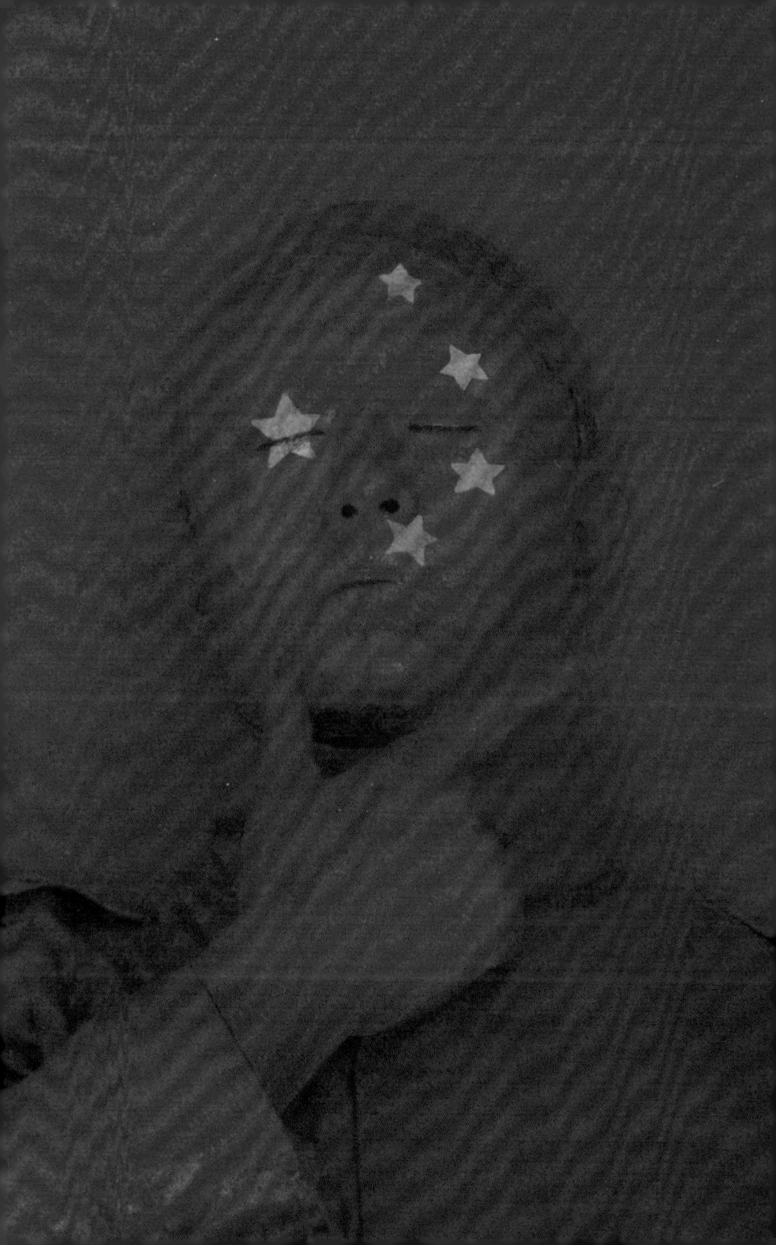

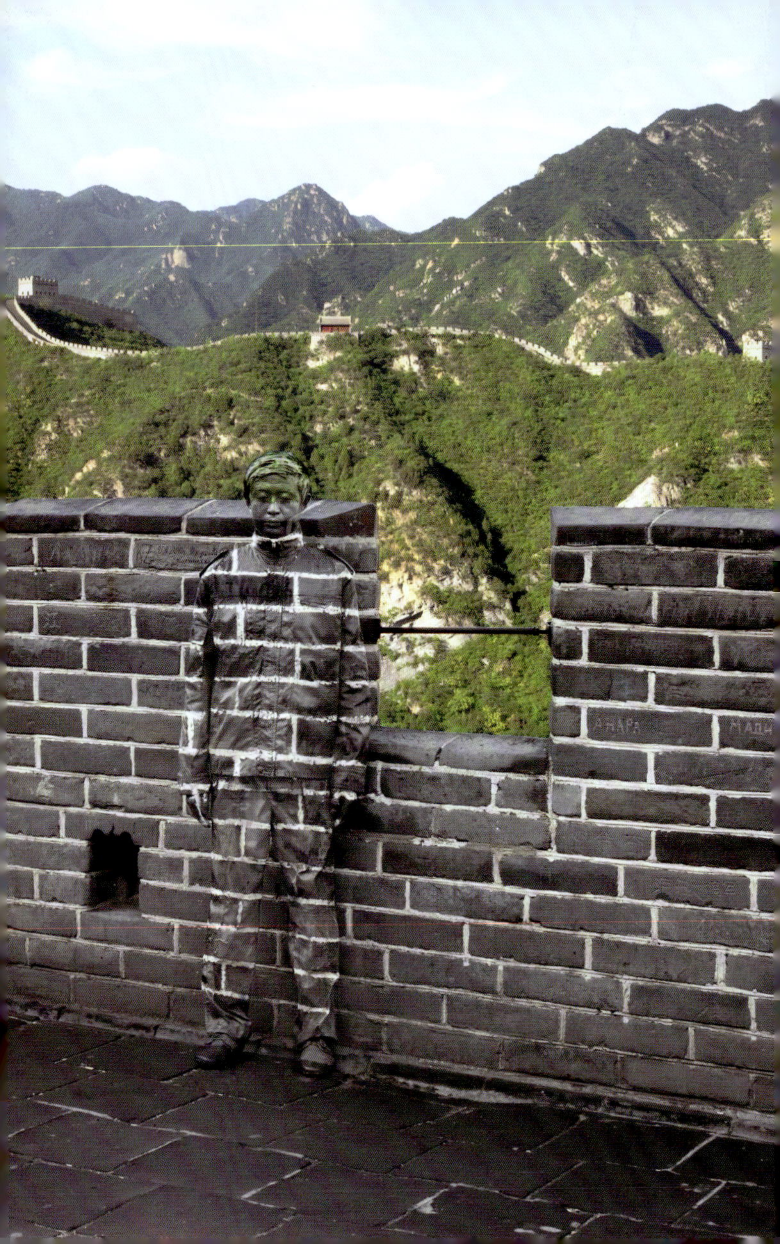

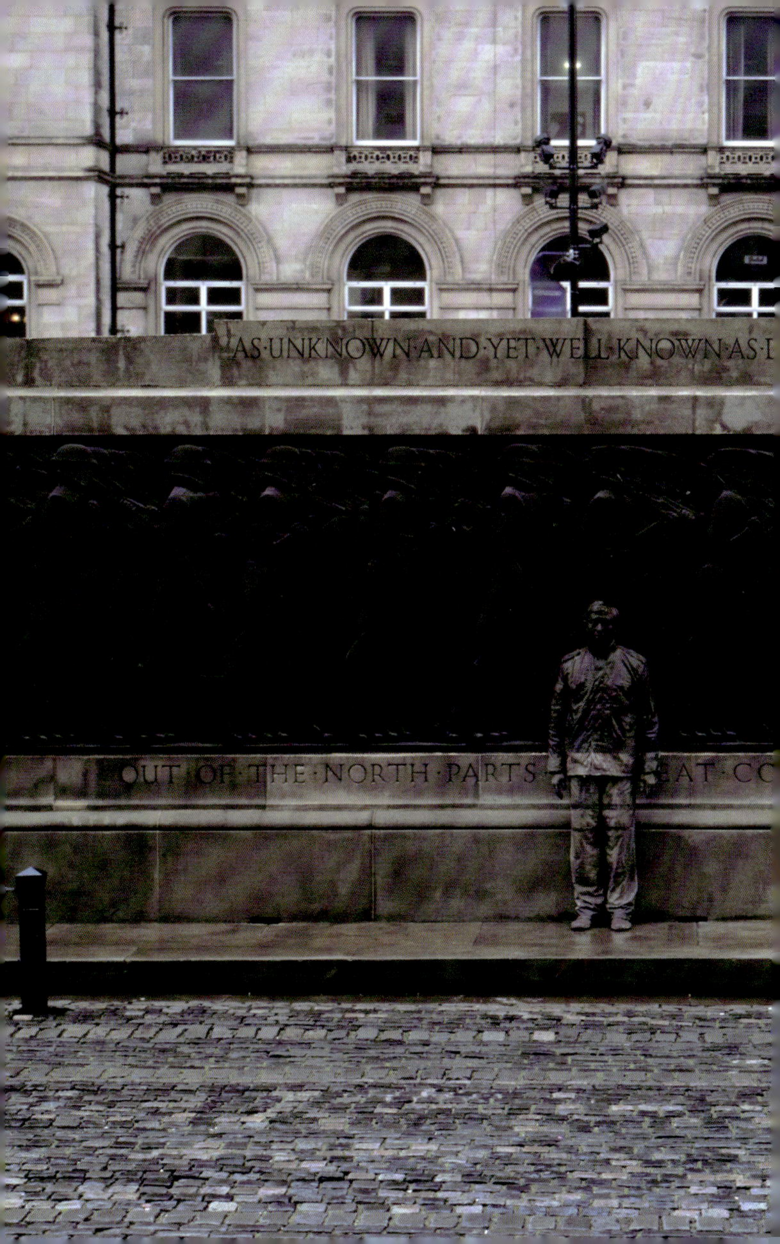
AS·UNKNOWN·AND·YET·WELL·KNOWN·AS·
OUT·OF·THE·NORTH·PARTS

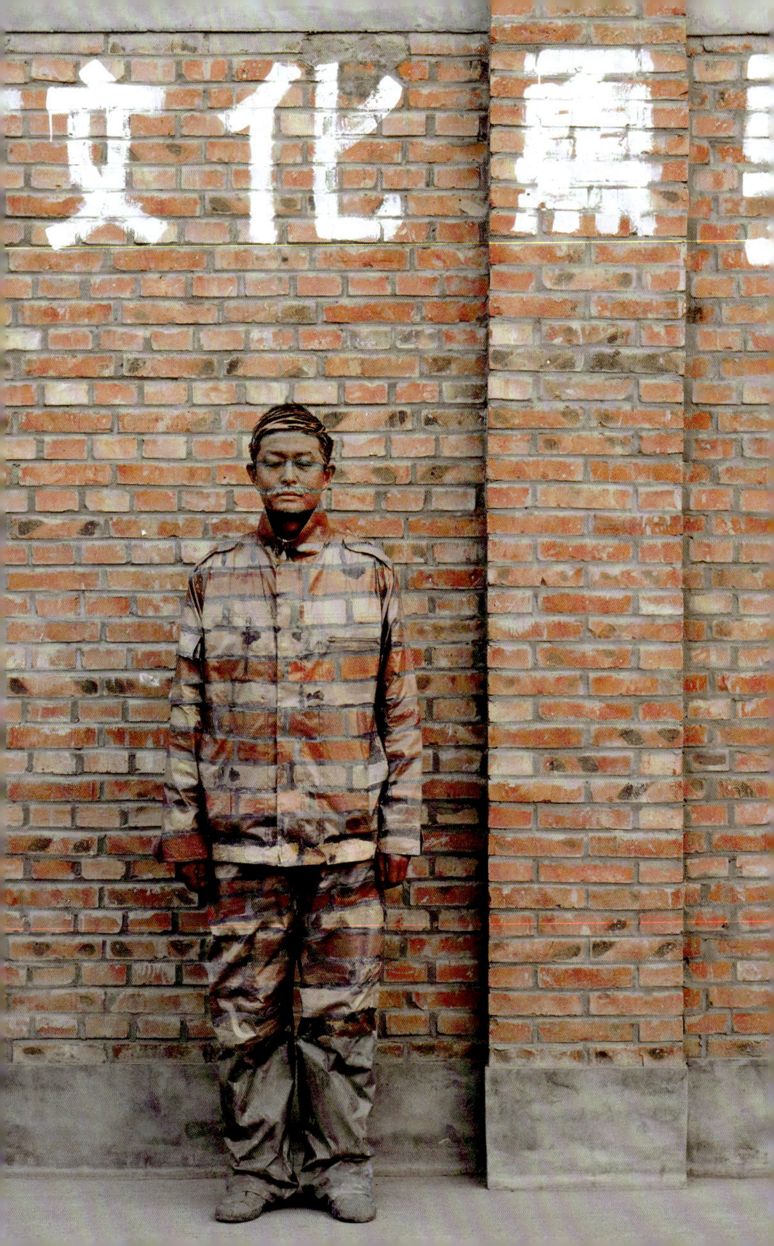
文化

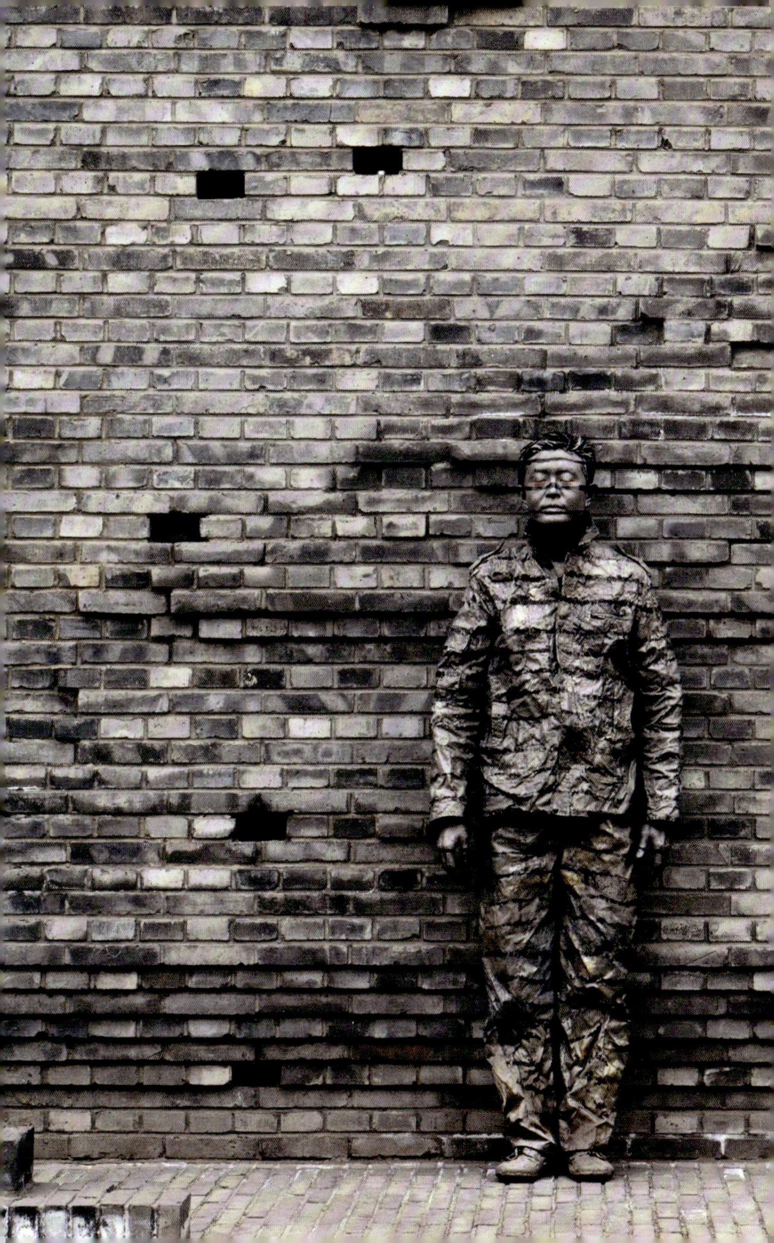

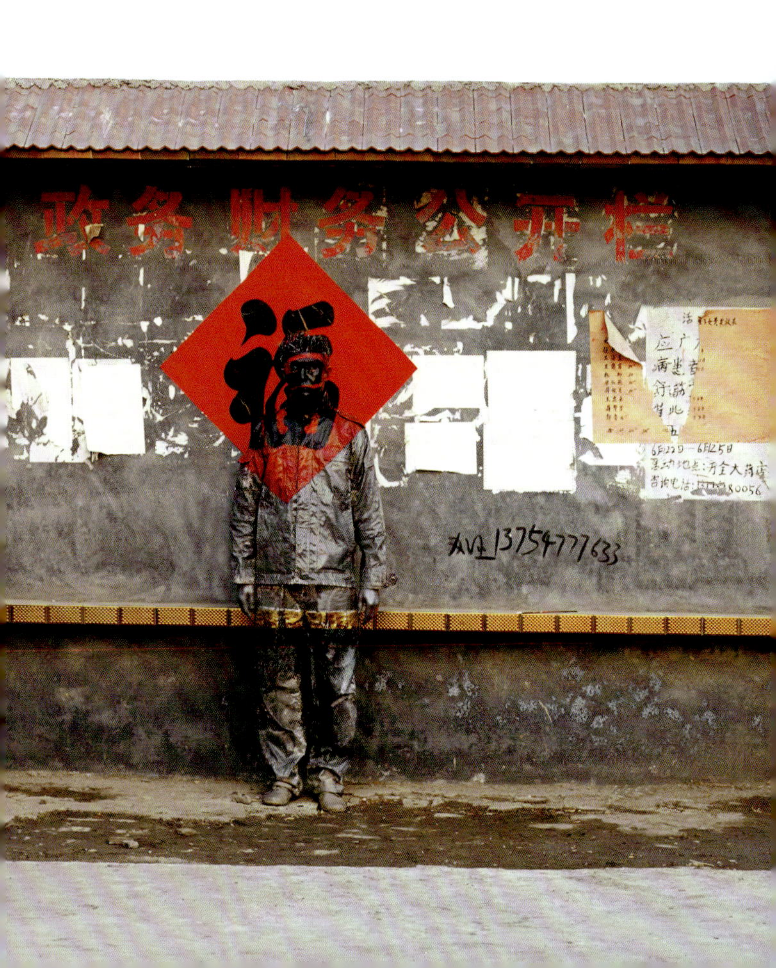
政务财务公开栏
福
办证13754777633

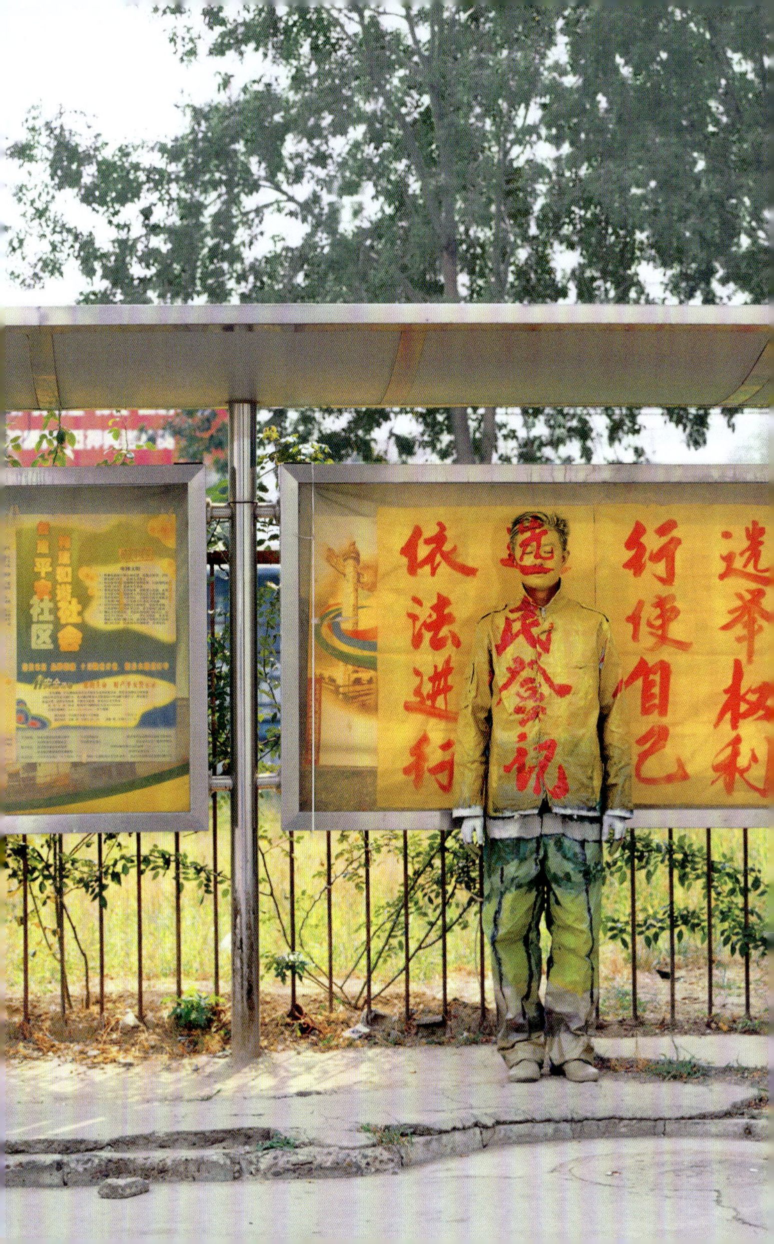

平安
社区
和谐社会
依法进行
行使自己
选举权利

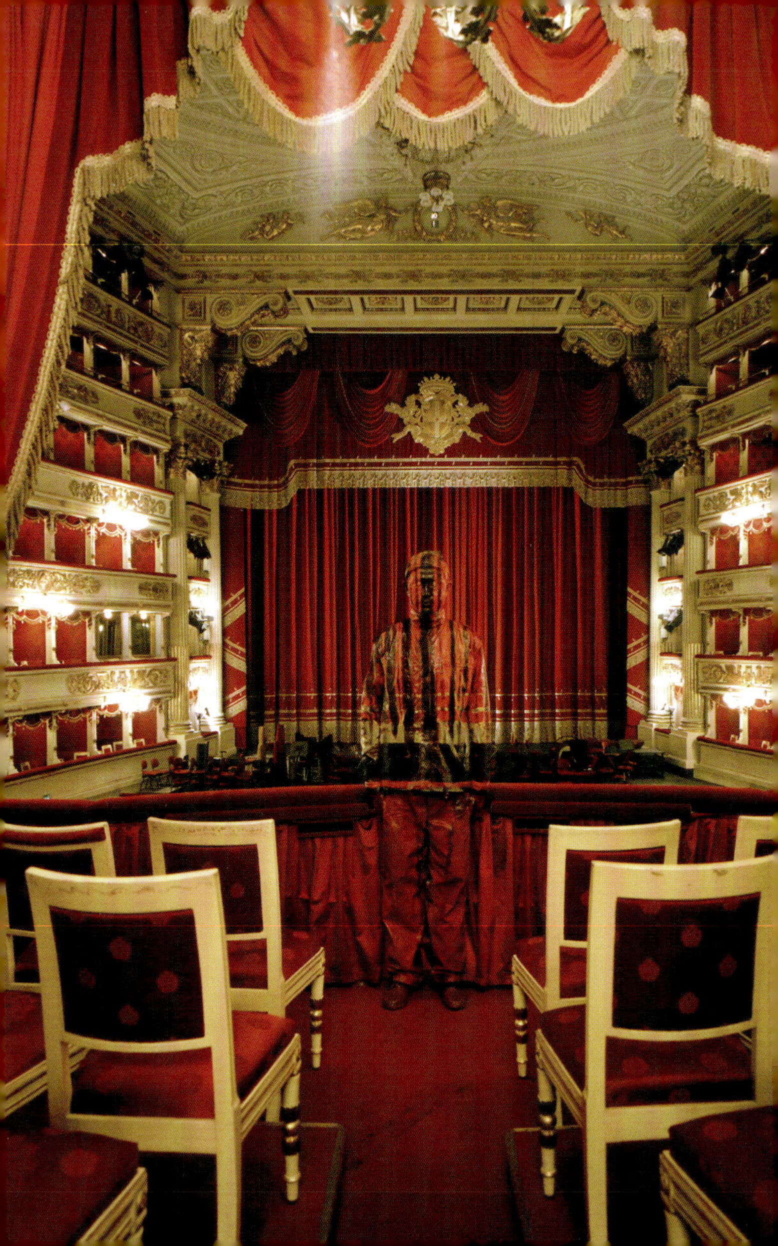

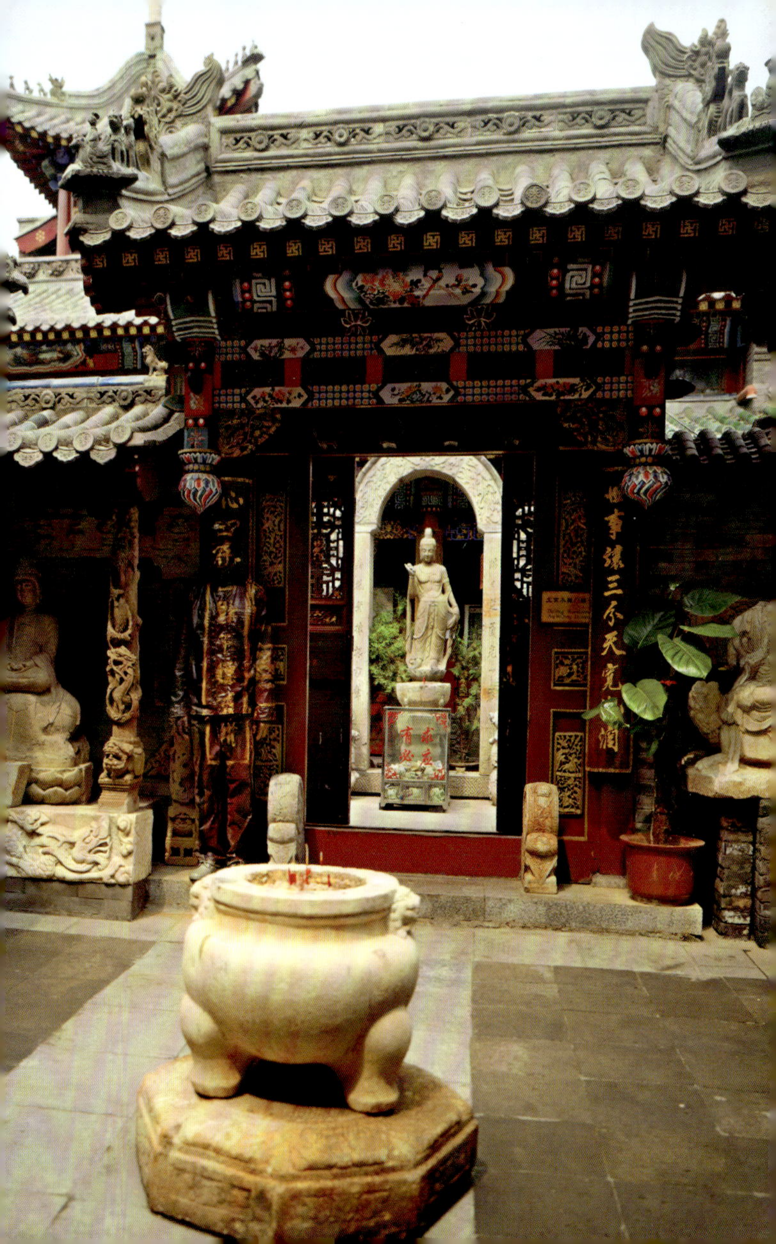
有求必应

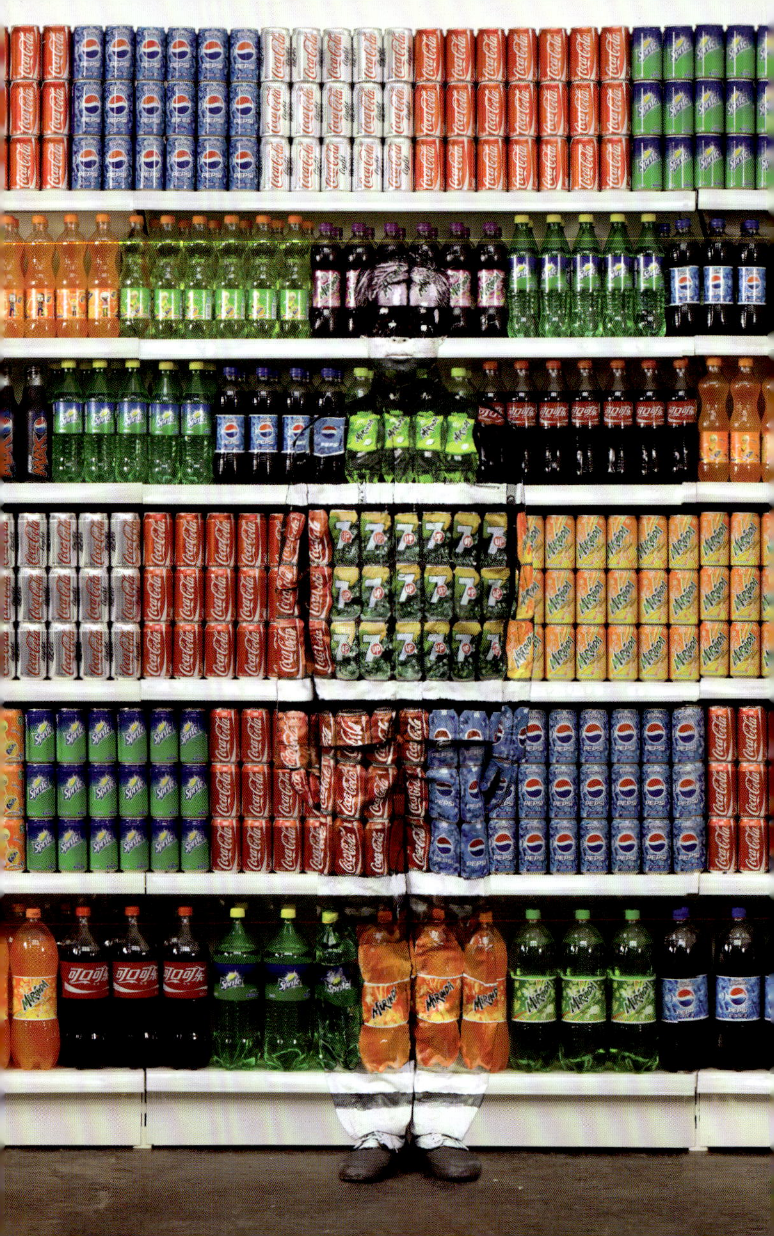

Coca-Cola
PEPSI
Sprite
Mirinda
7up
可口可乐

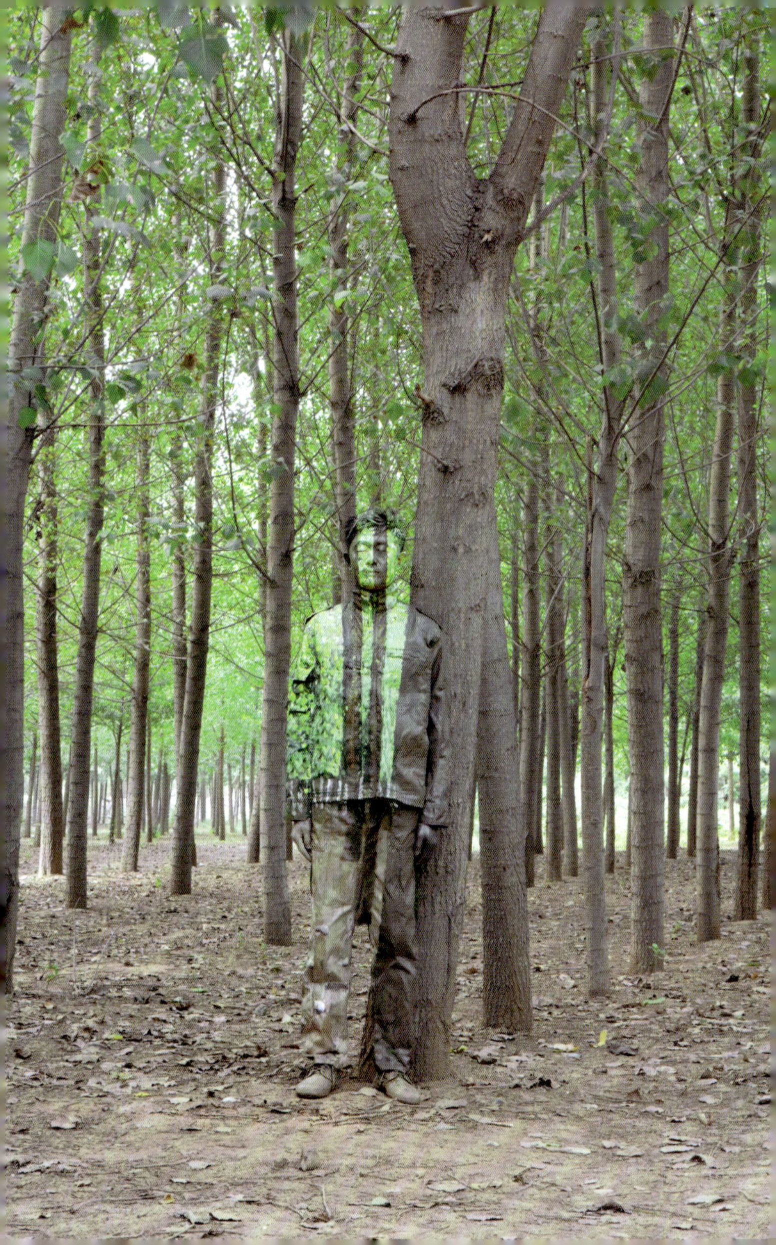

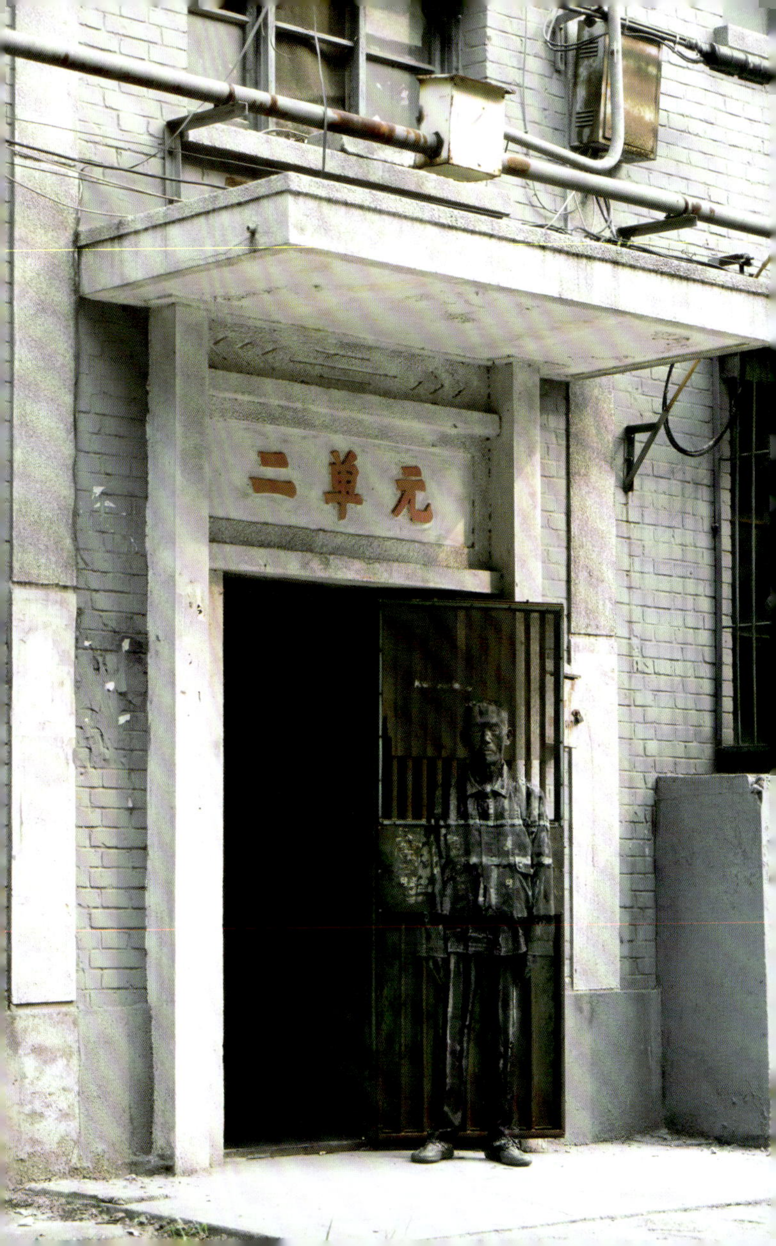
二単元

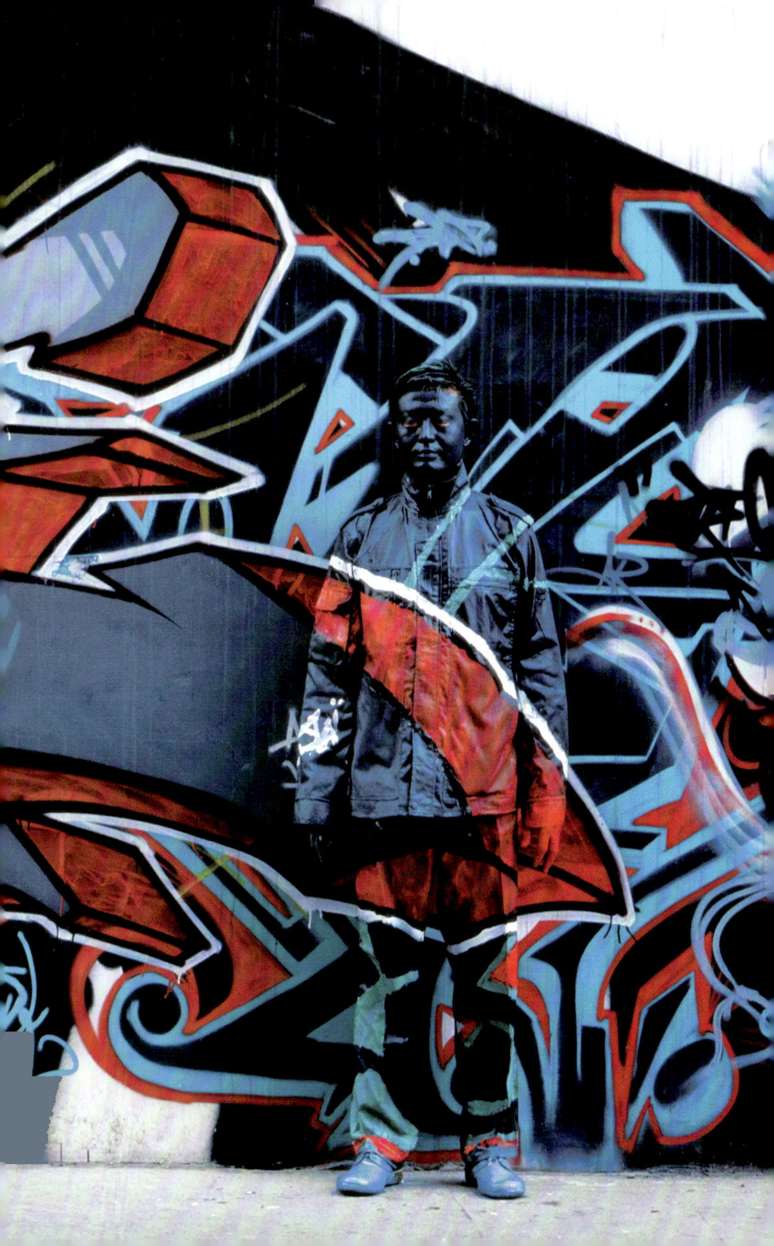

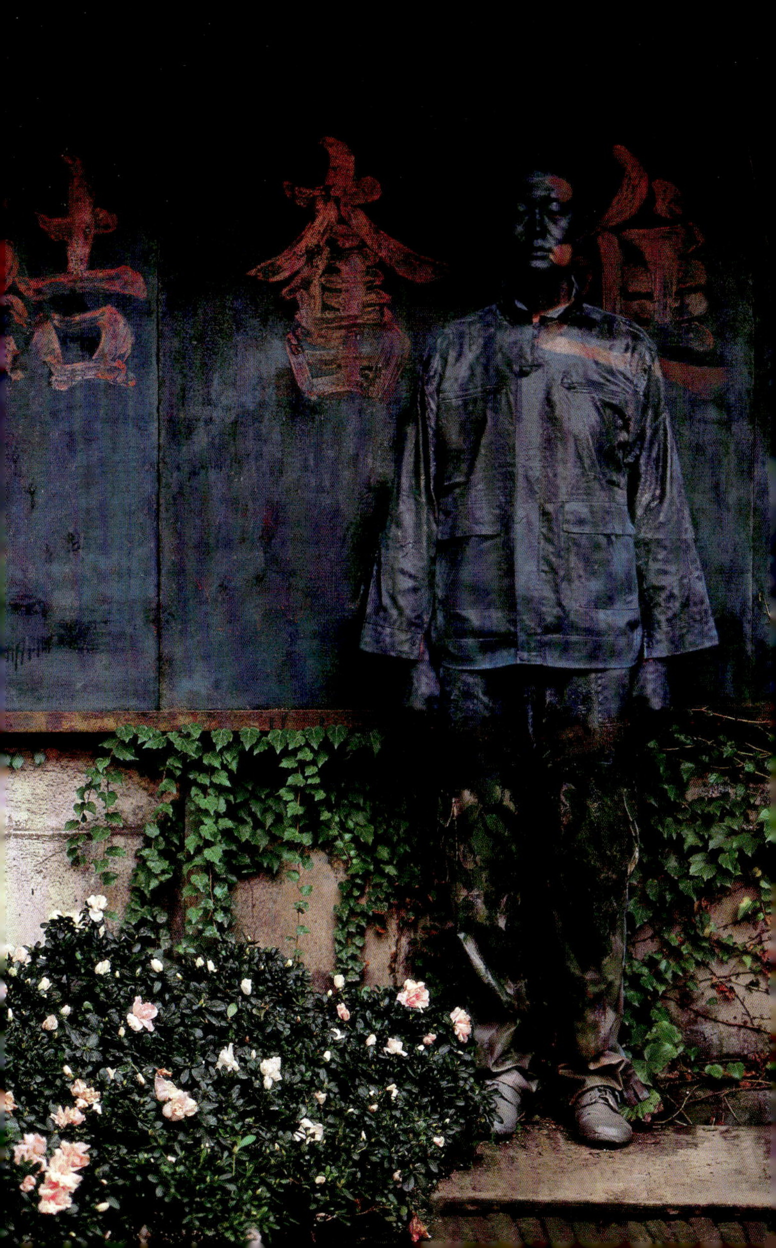

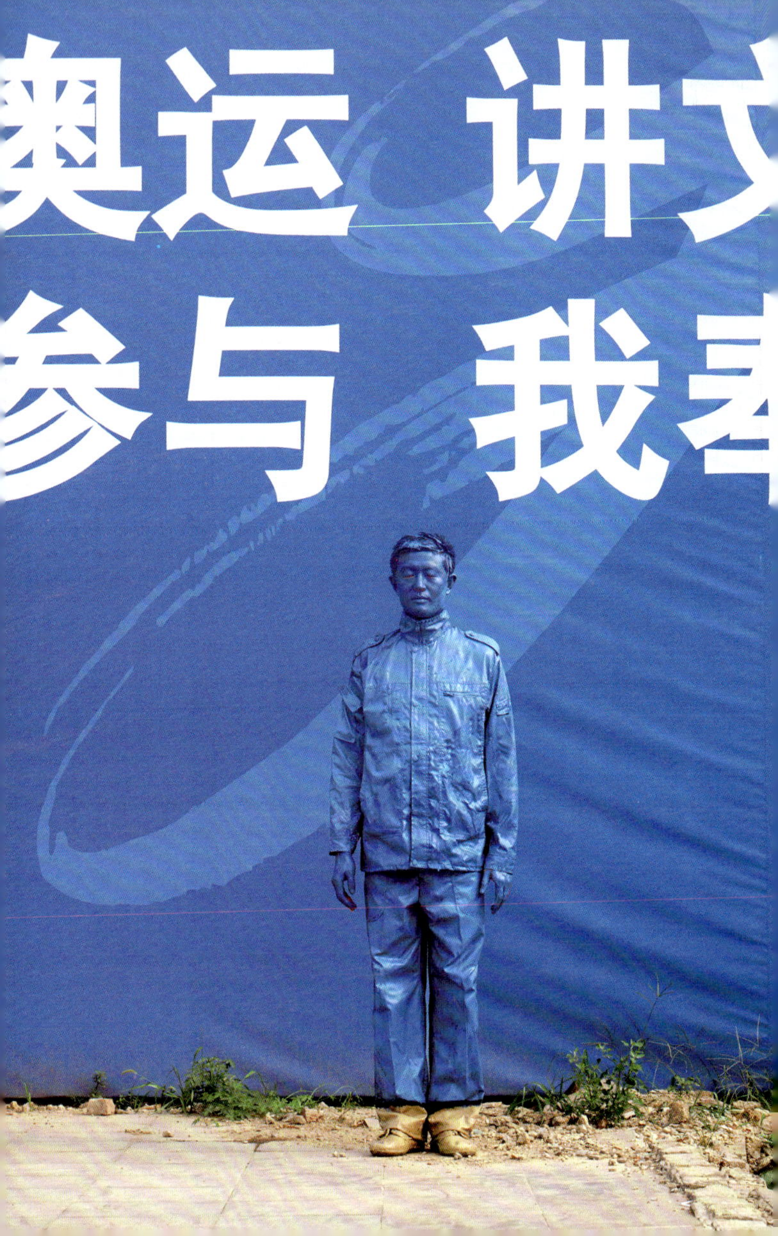
奥运 讲
参与 我

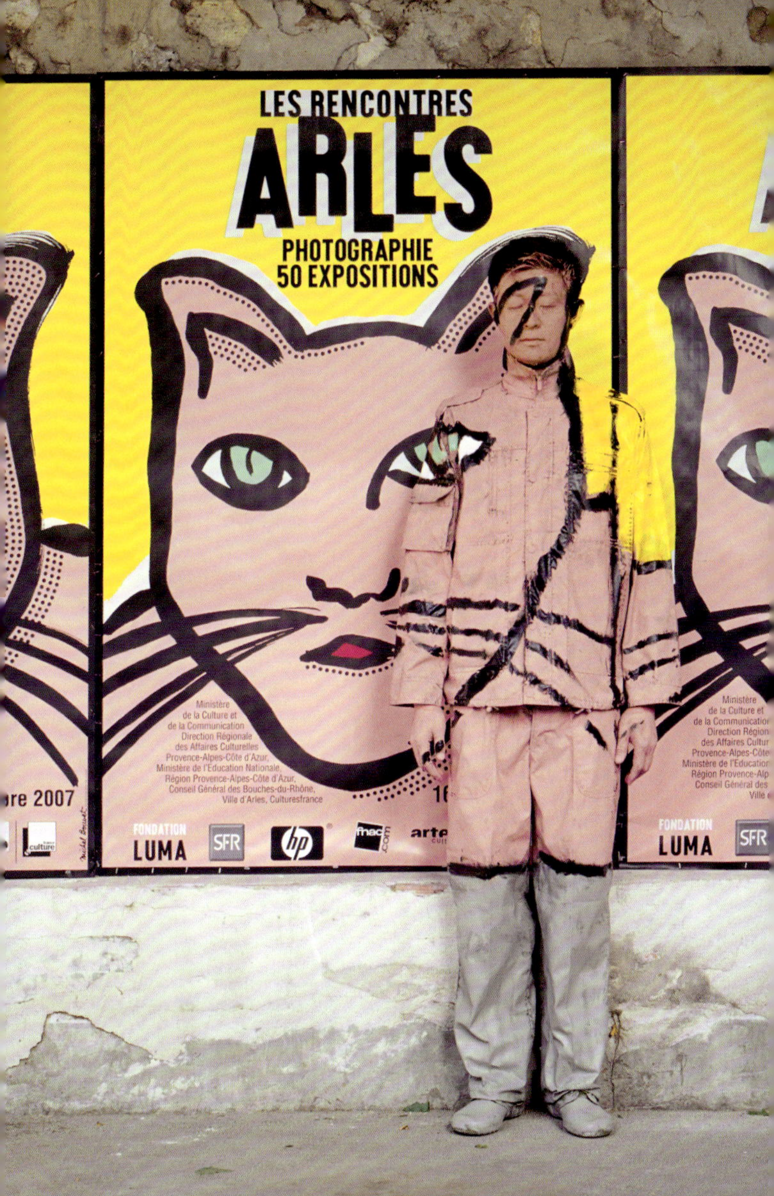
LES RENCONTRES
ARLES
PHOTOGRAPHIE
50 EXPOSITIONS
Ministère
de la Culture et
de la Communication
Direction Régionale
des Affaires Culturelles
Provence-Alpes-Côte d'Azur,
Ministère de l'Education Nationale,
Région Provence-Alpes-Côte d'Azur,
Conseil Général des Bouches-du-Rhône,
Ville d'Arles, Culturesfrance
FONDATION
LUMA
SFR
hp
fnac.com
arte

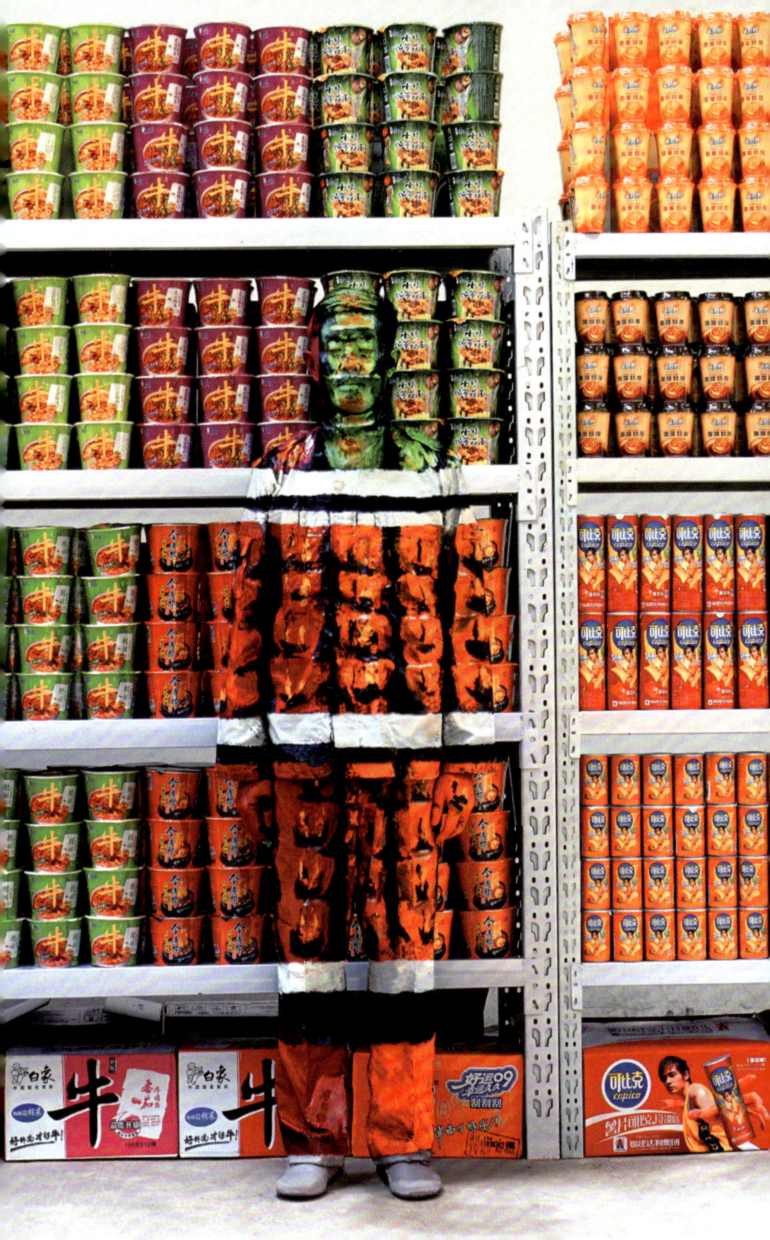
白象
牛
白象
牛
刮刮刮
可比克
copico

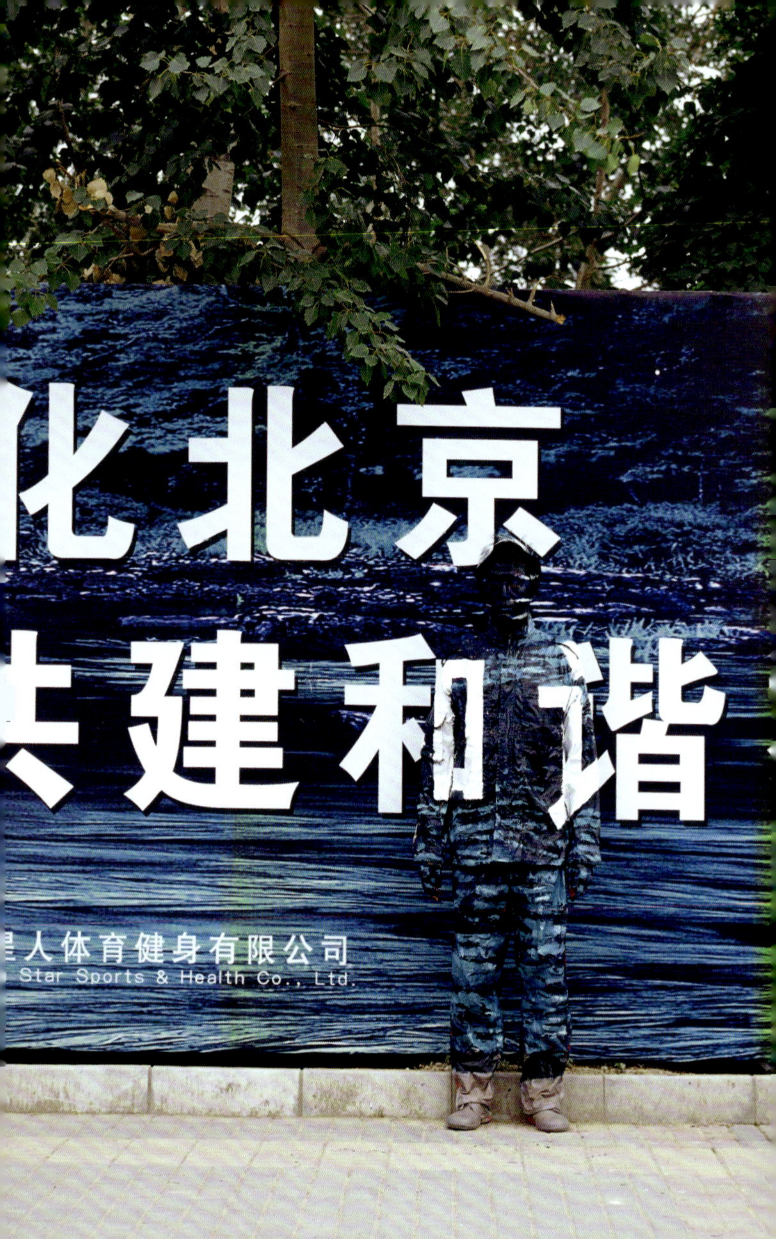
化北京
建和谐
人体育健身有限公司
Star Sports & Health Co., Ltd.

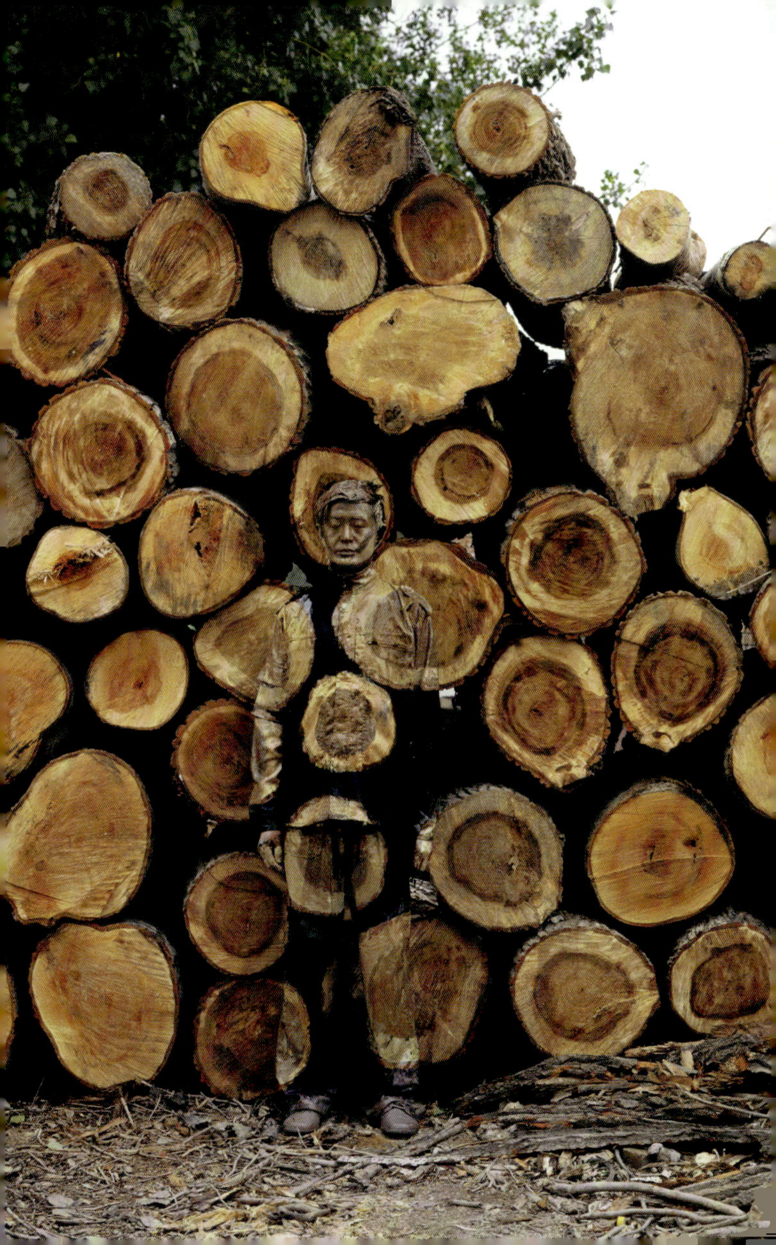

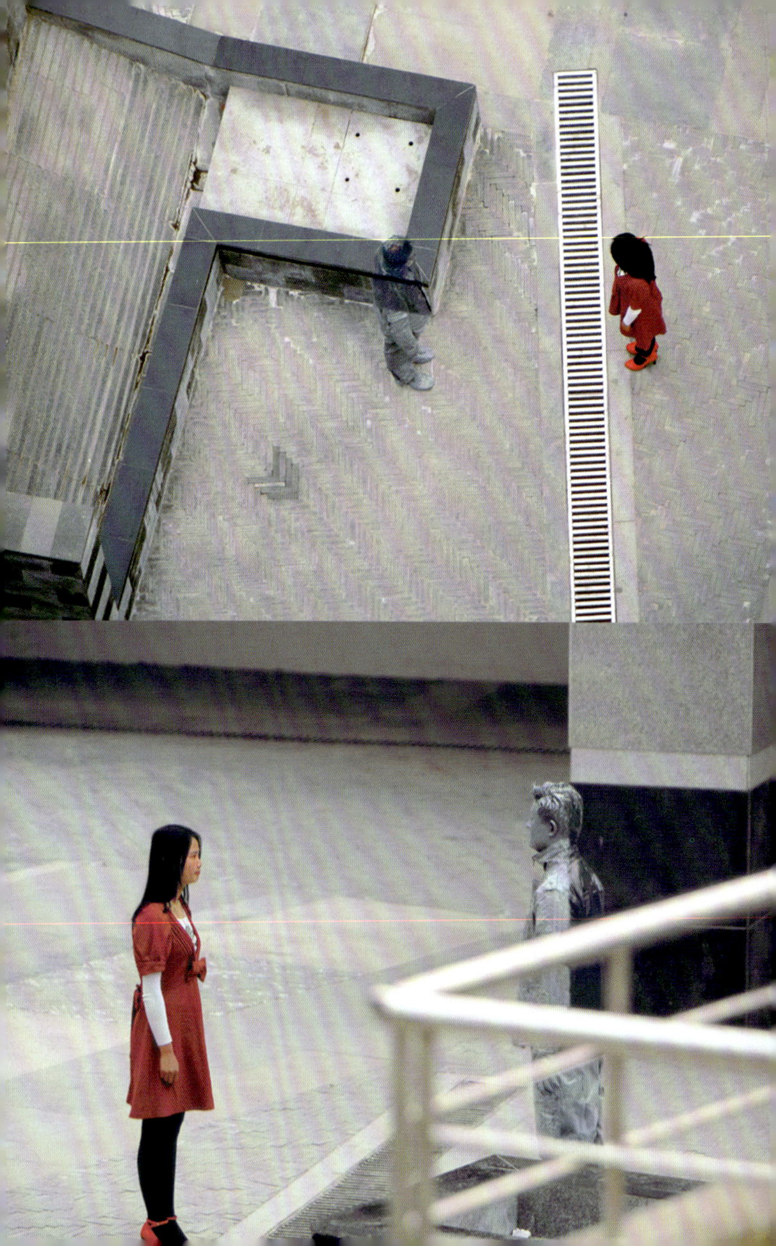

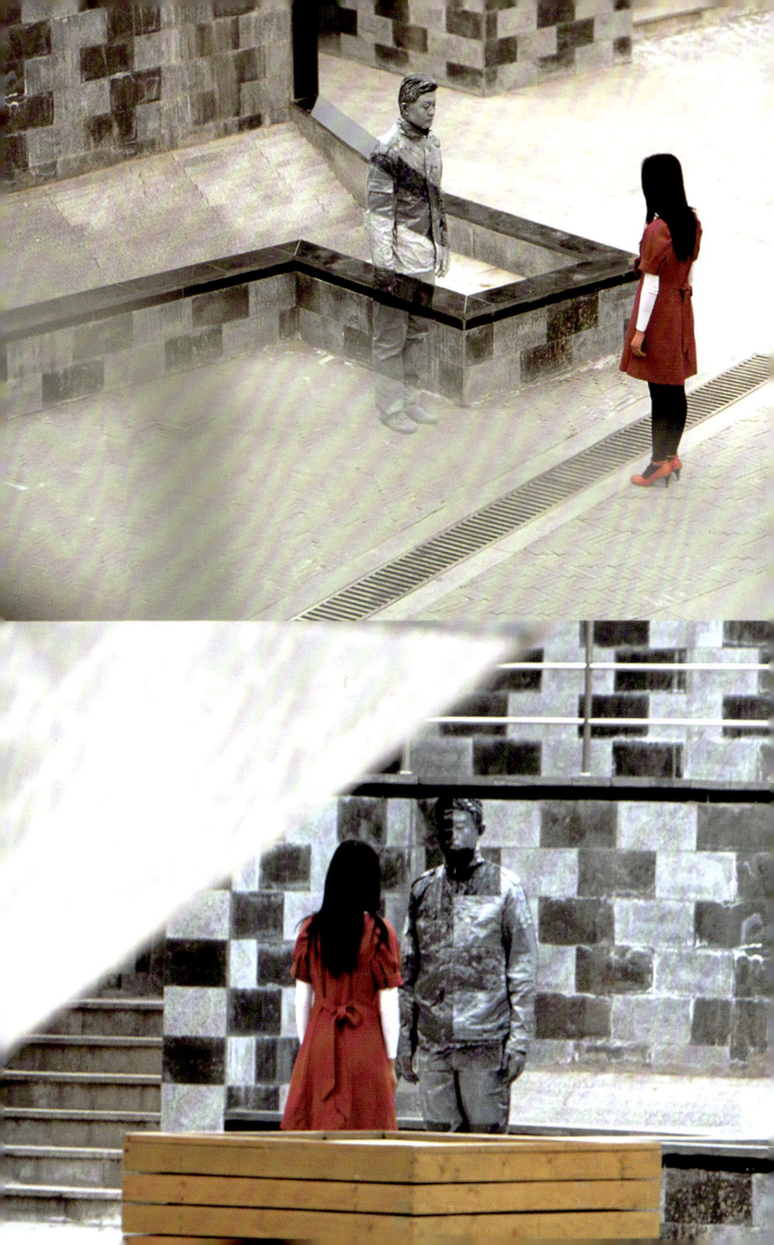

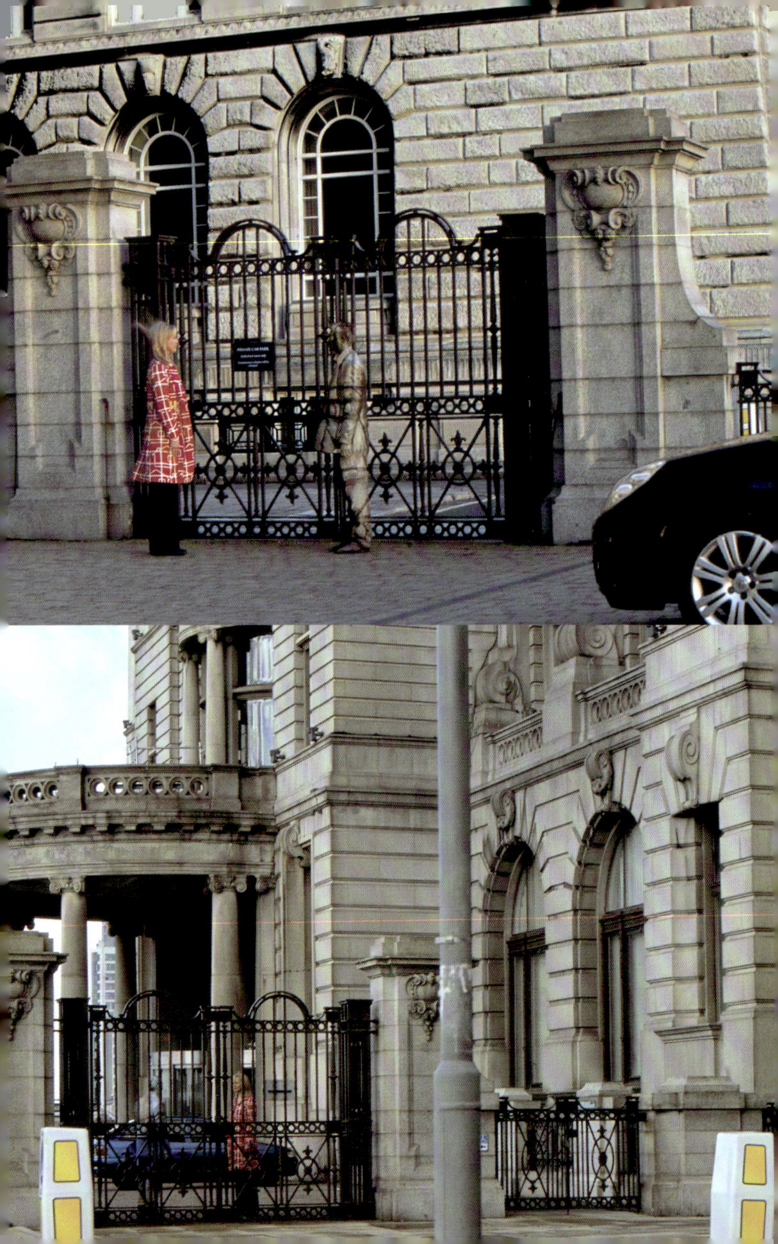
PRIVATE CAR PARK

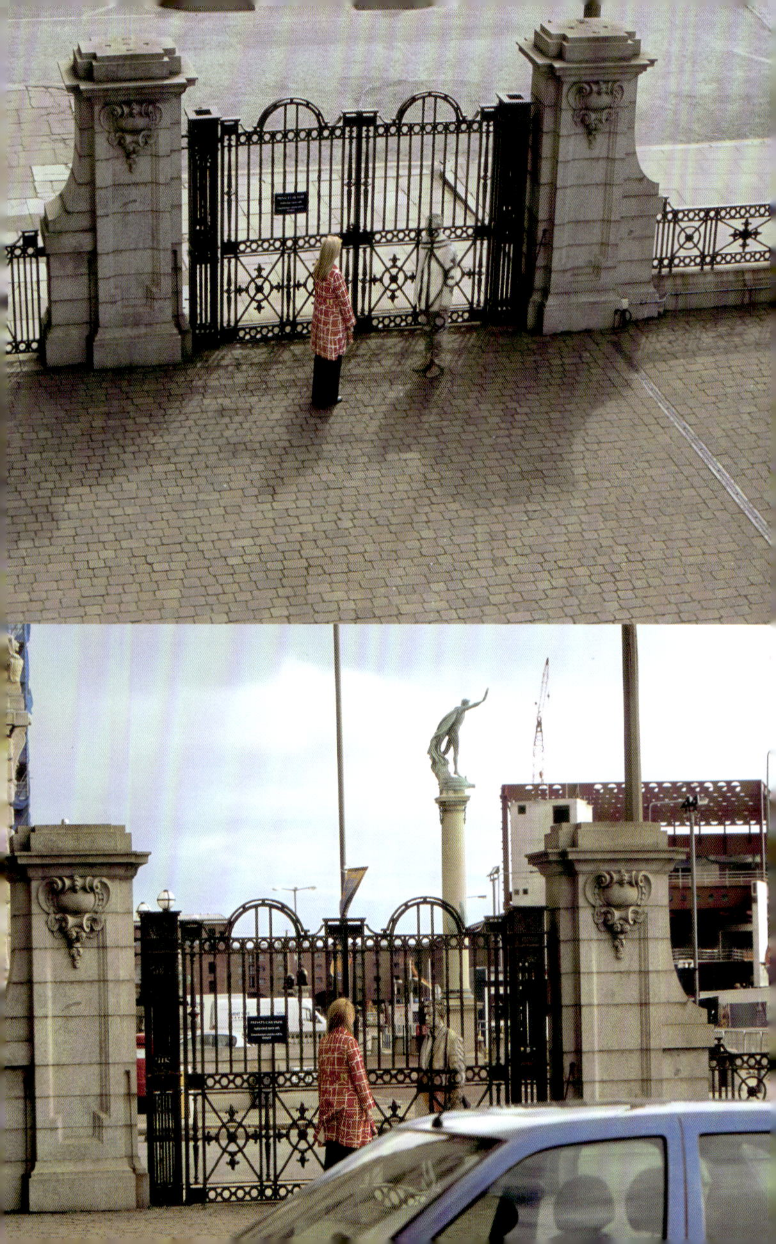
PRIVATE CAR PARK

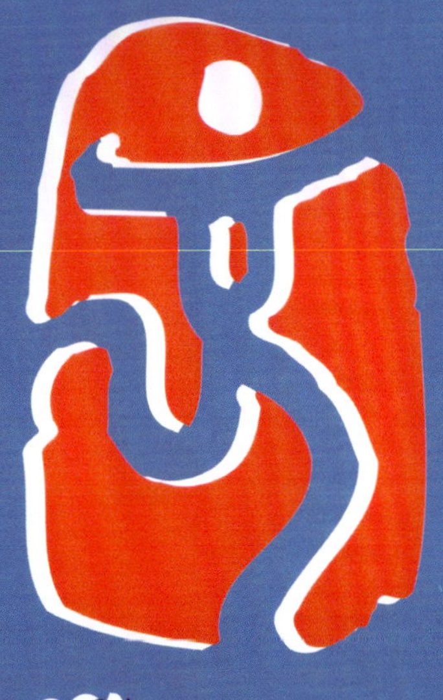

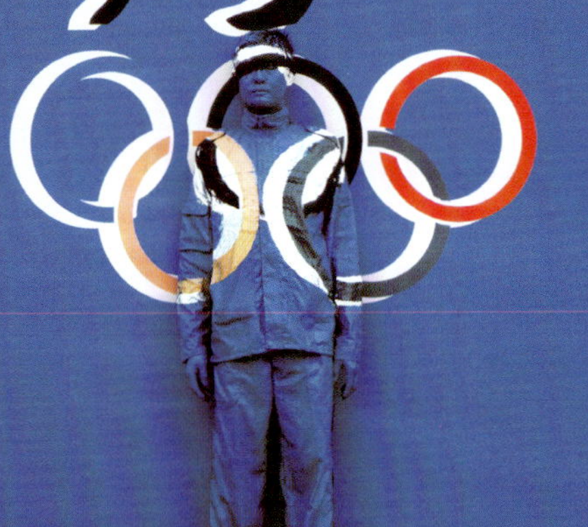
Beijing 2008

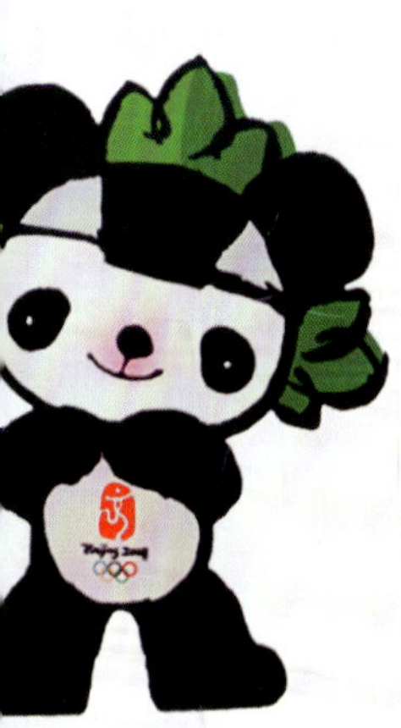
福娃晶晶
Jingjing

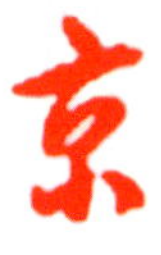
京

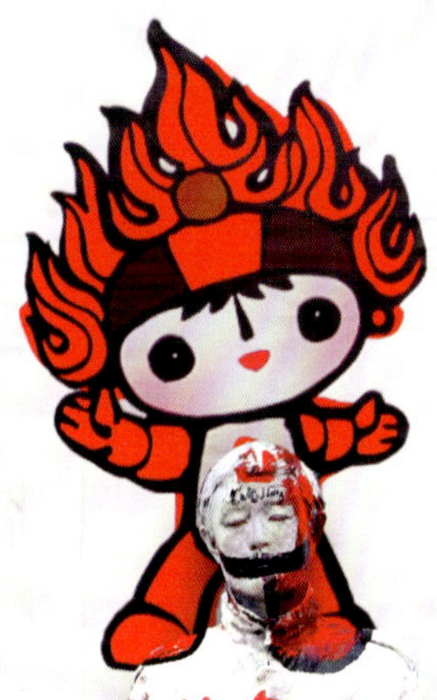
娃欢欢
欢

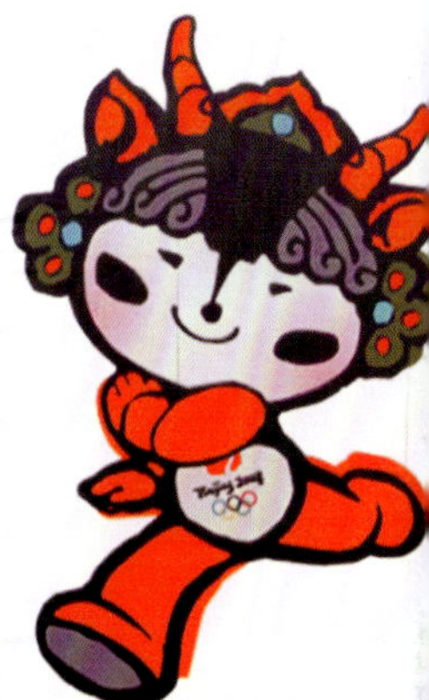
福娃迎迎
Yingying

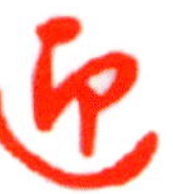
迎

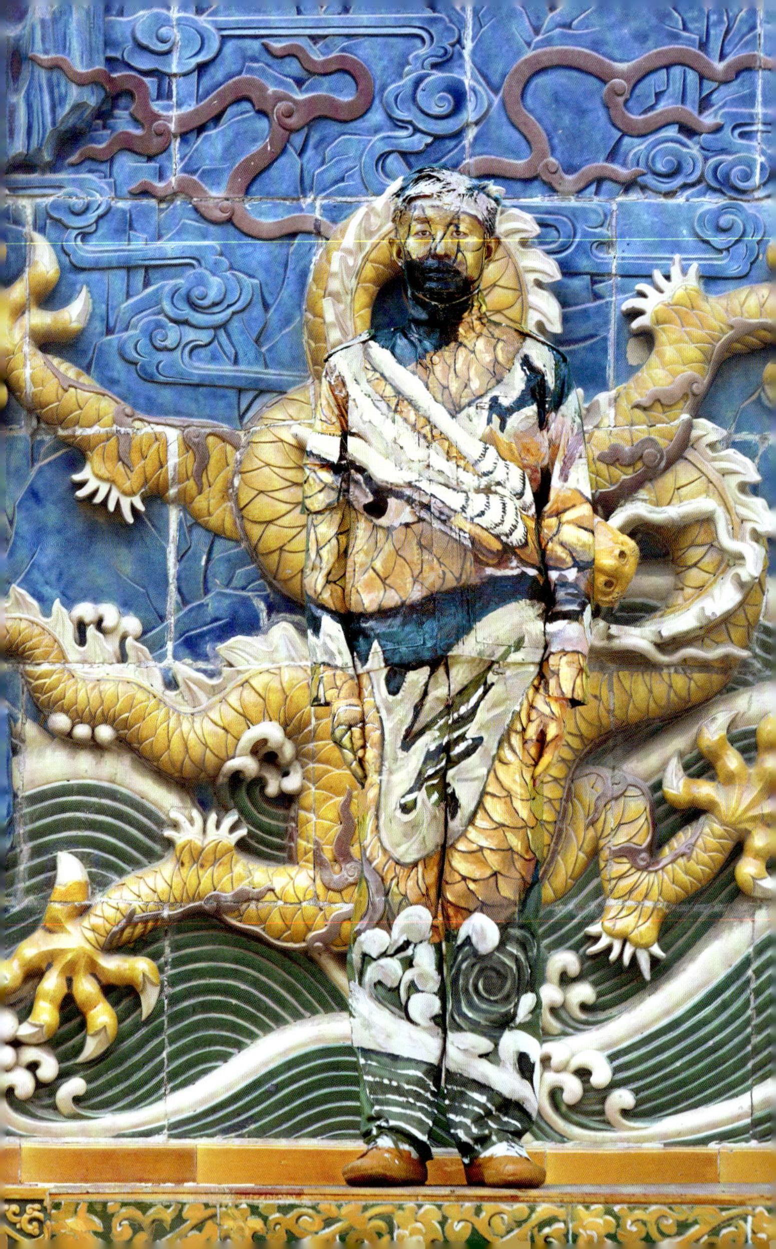

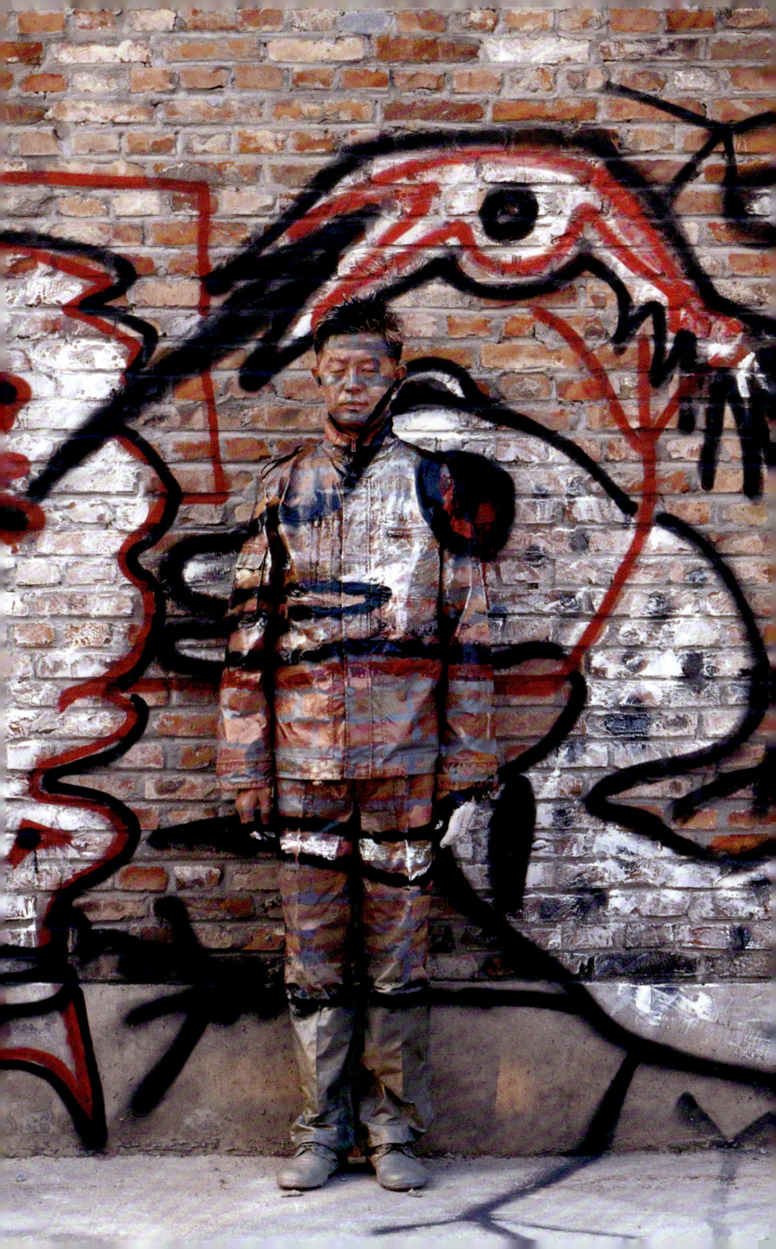

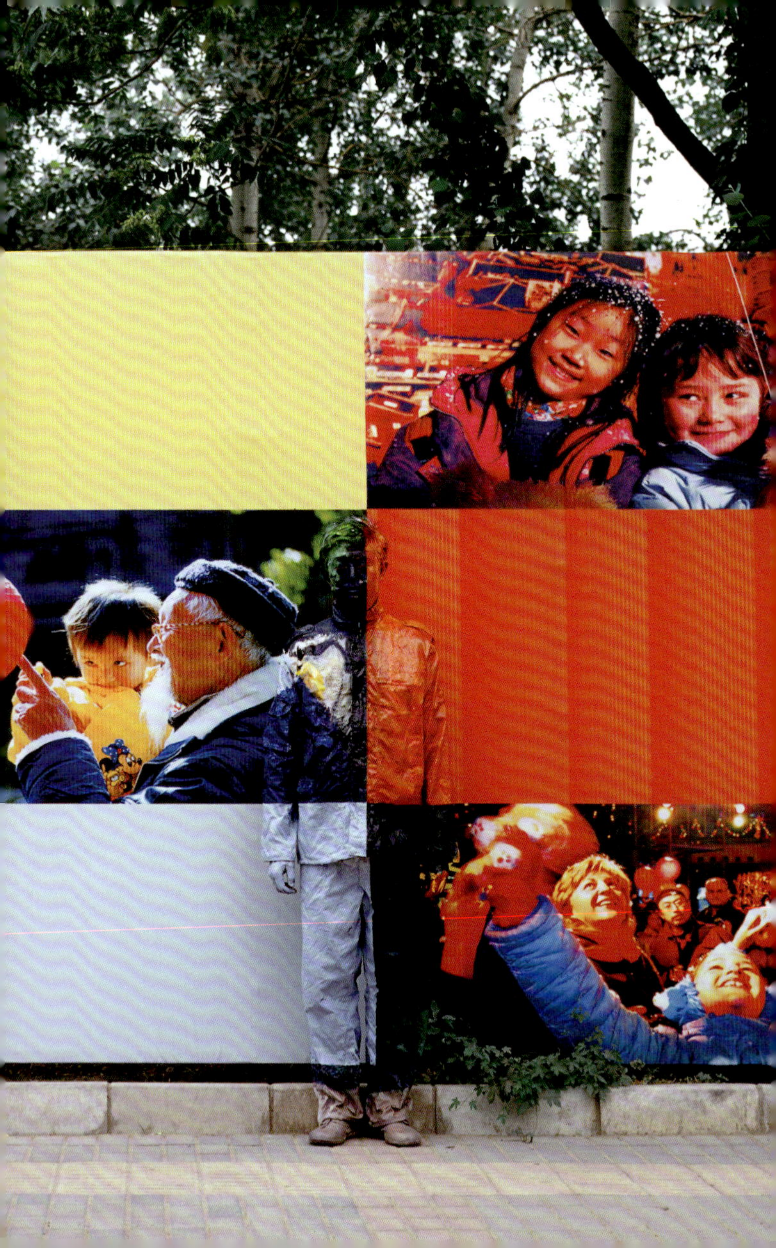

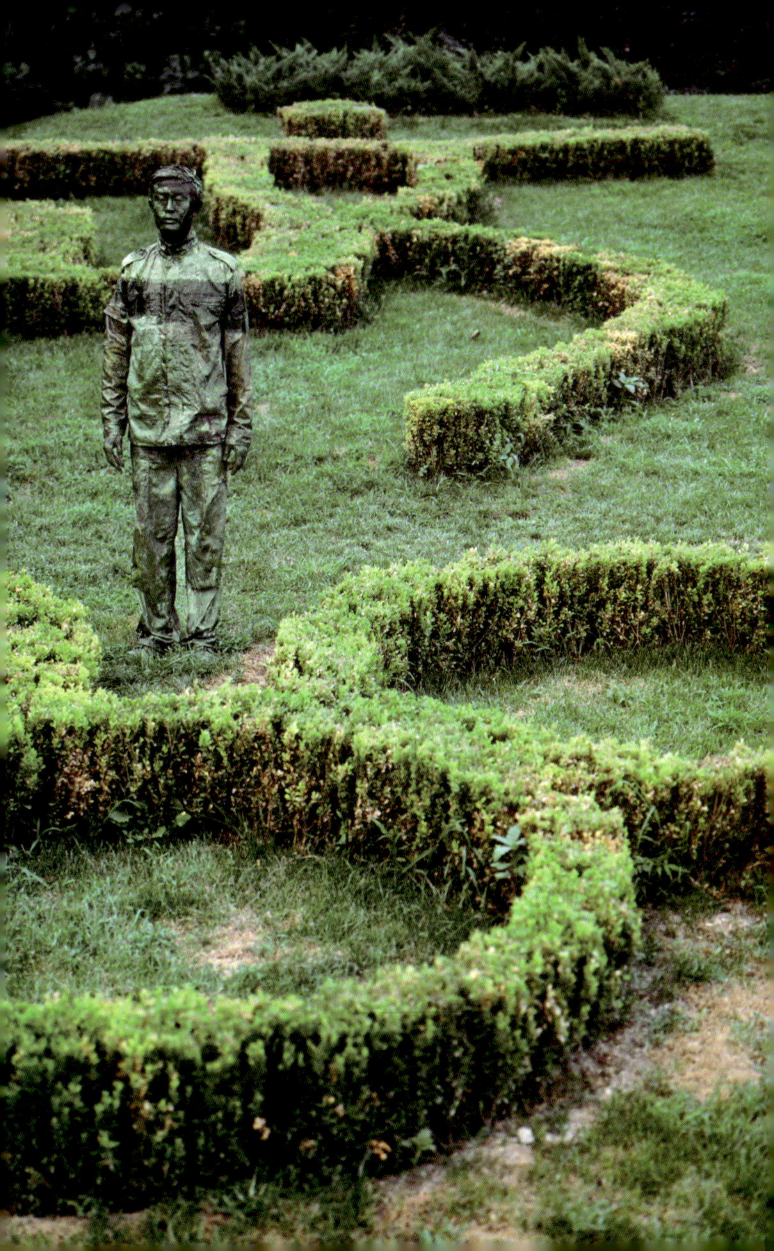

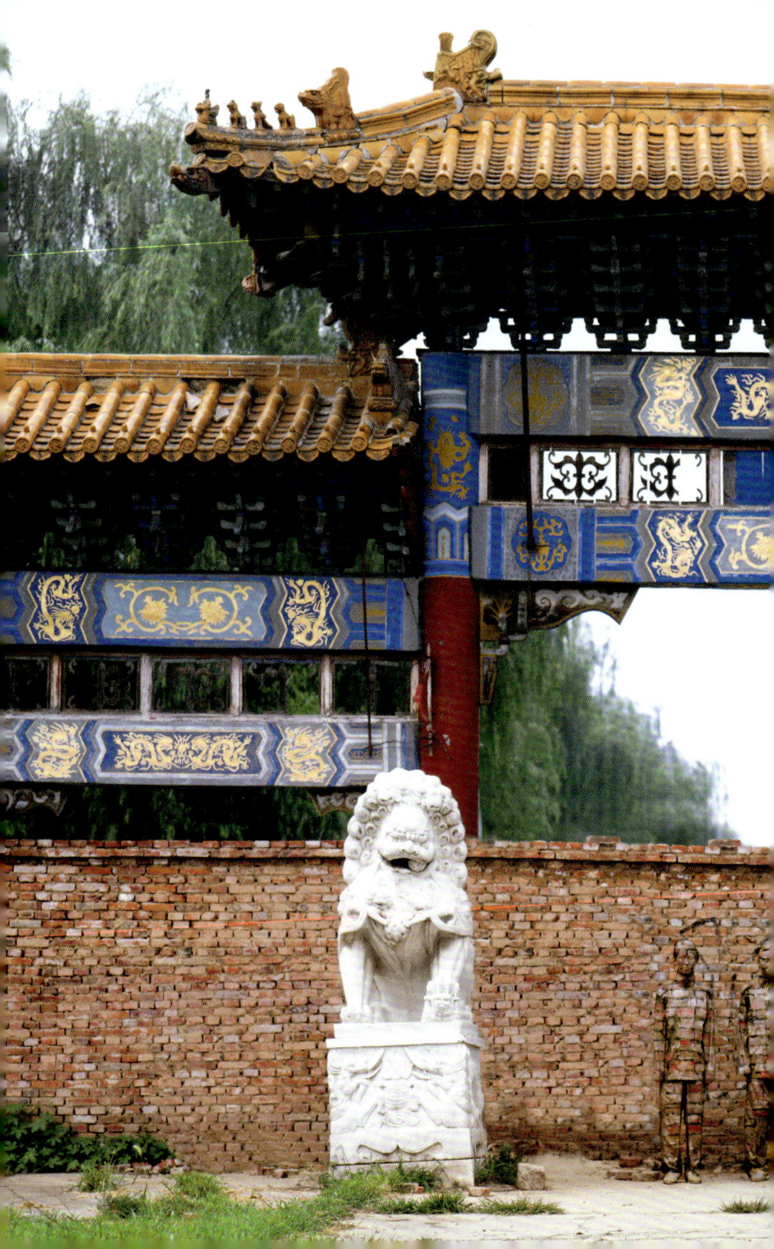

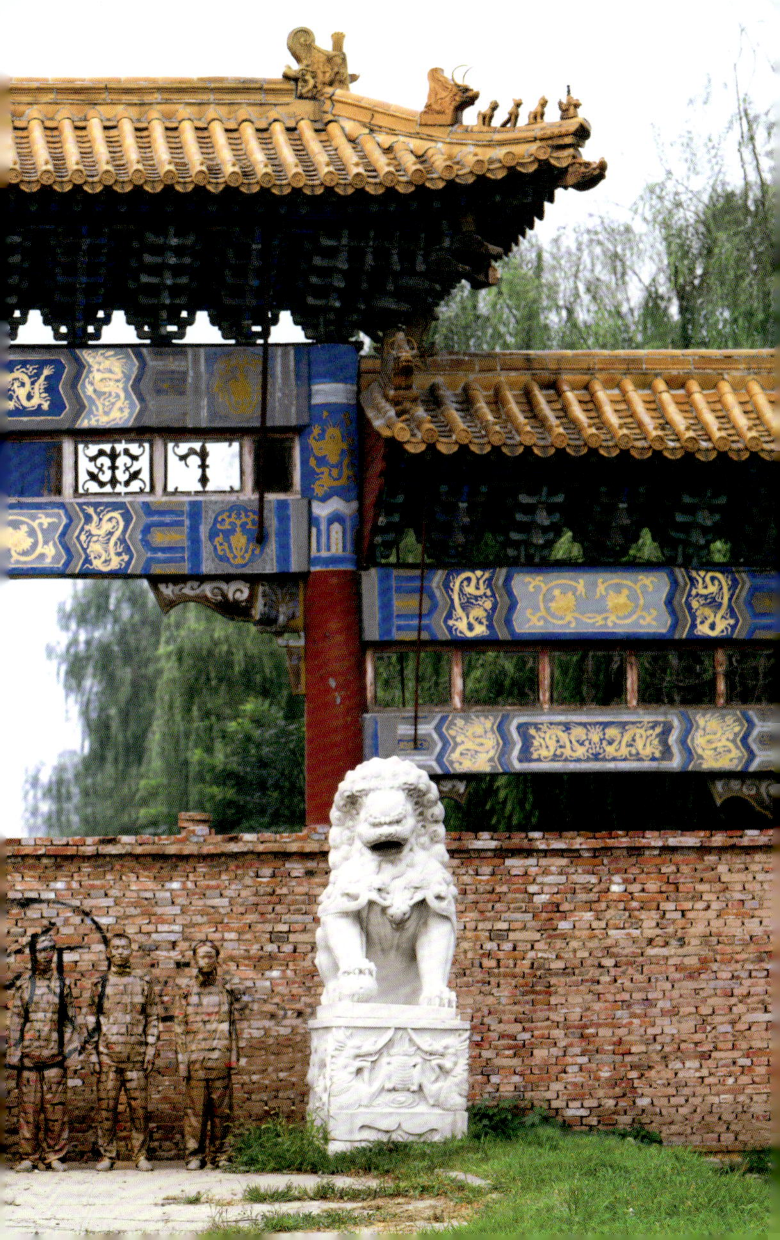

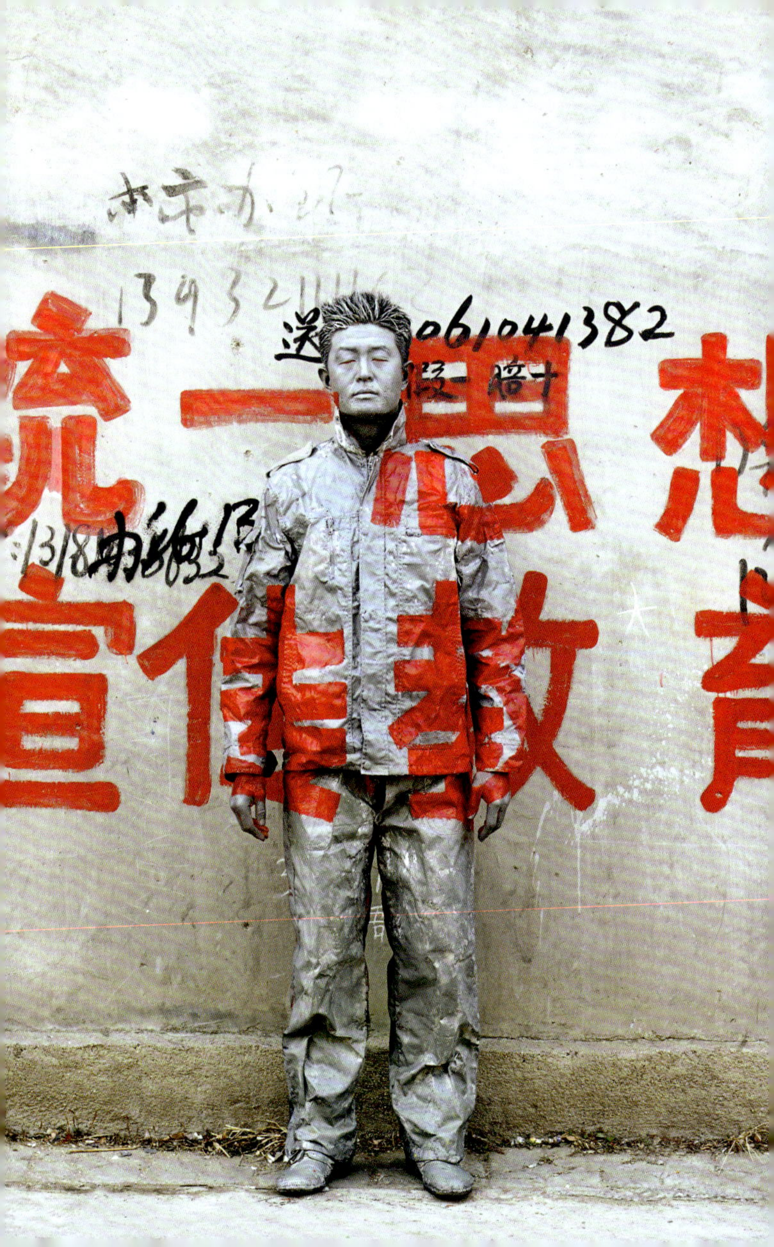

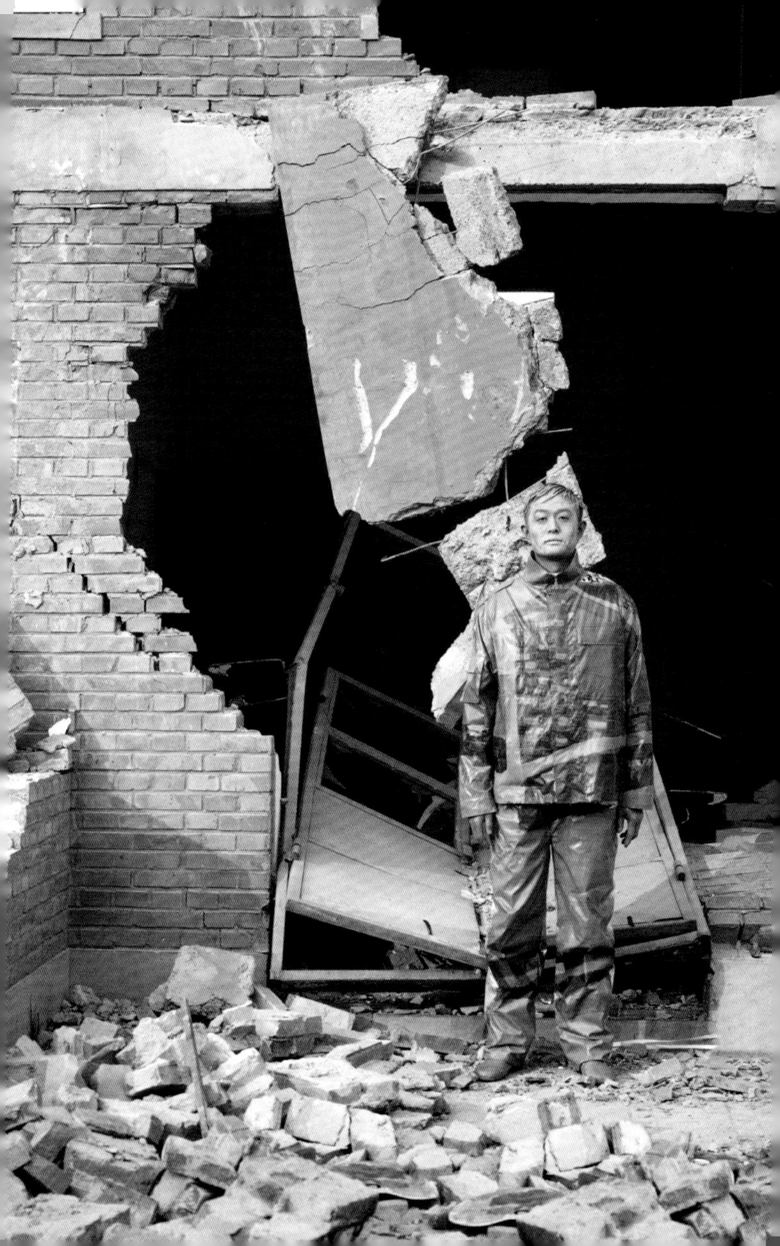

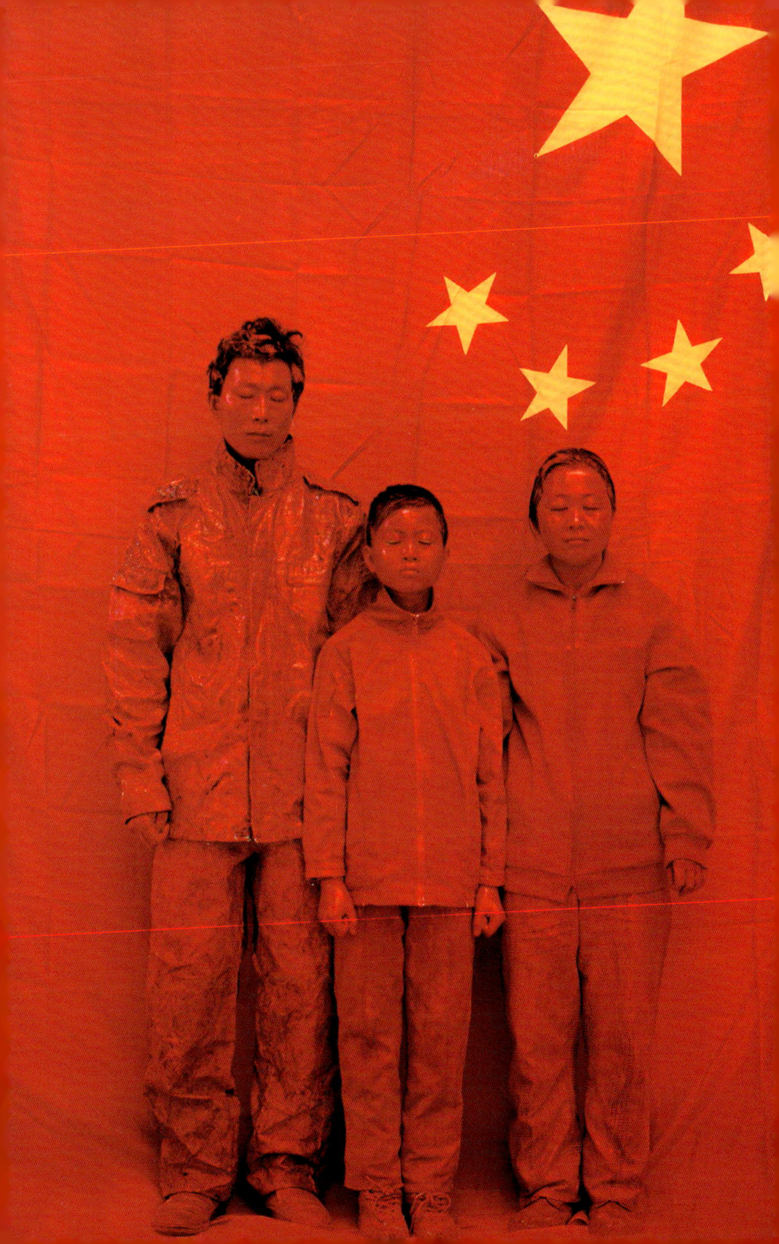

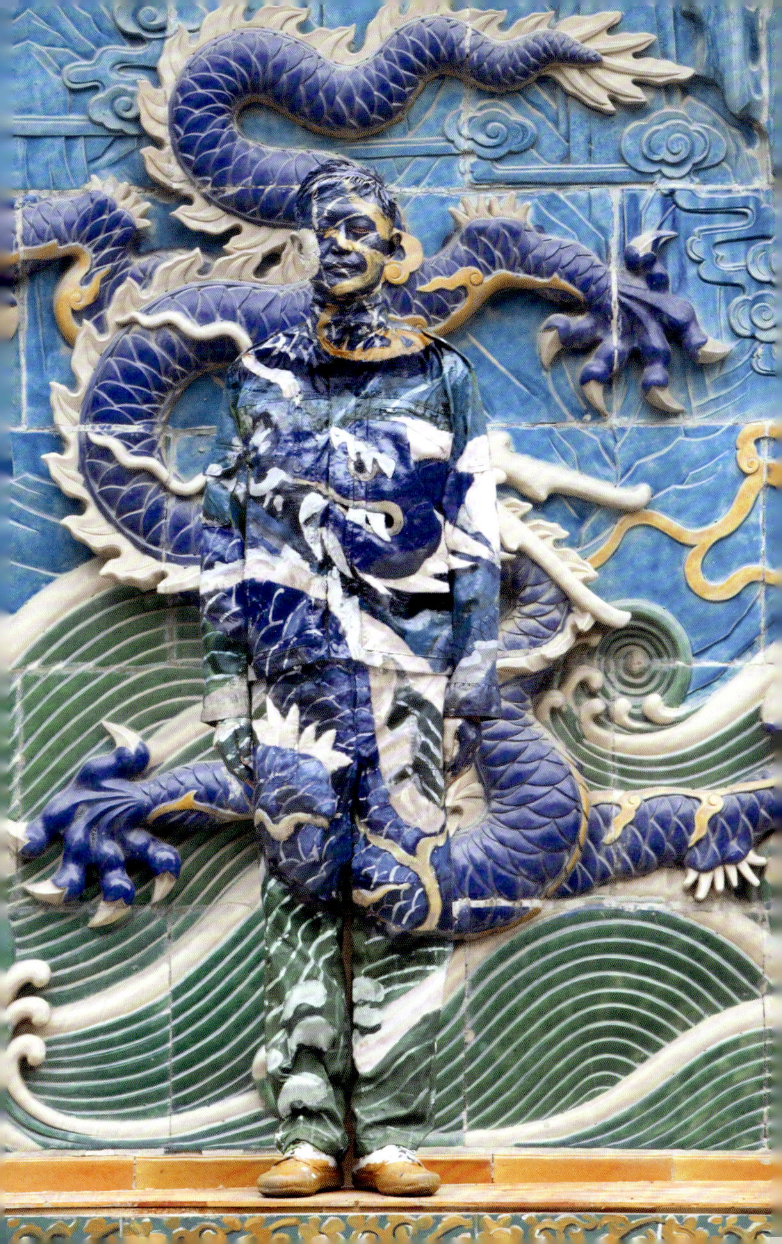

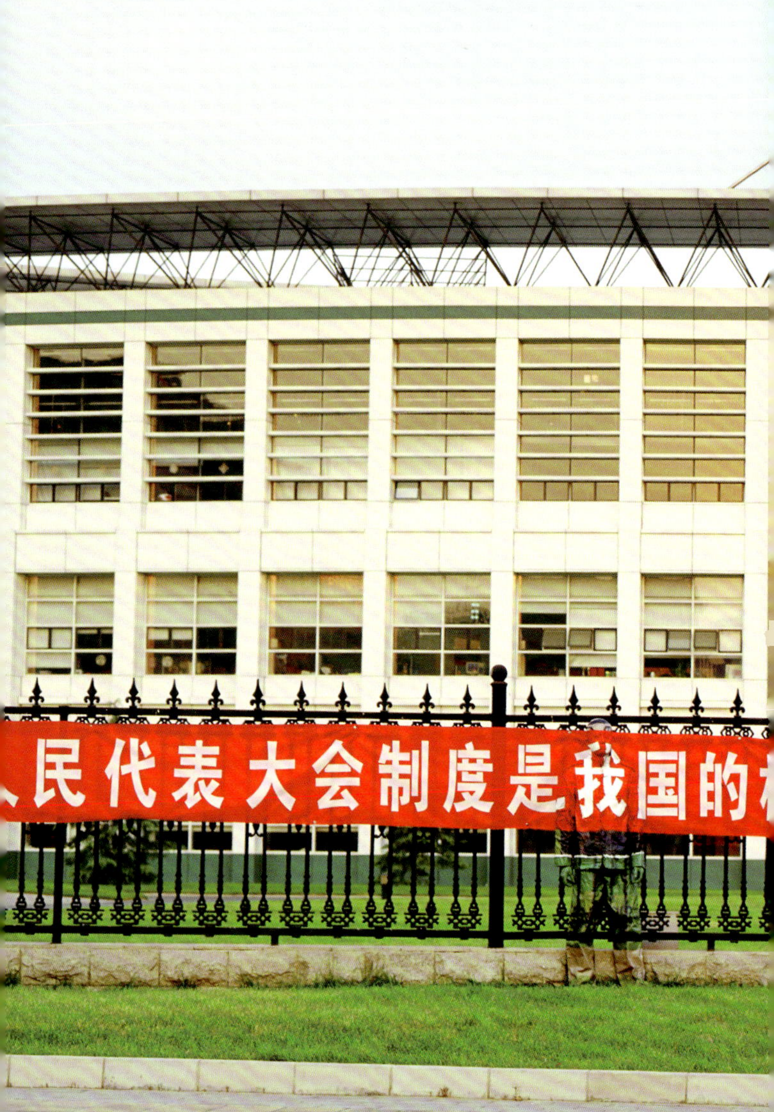
民代表大会制度是我国的

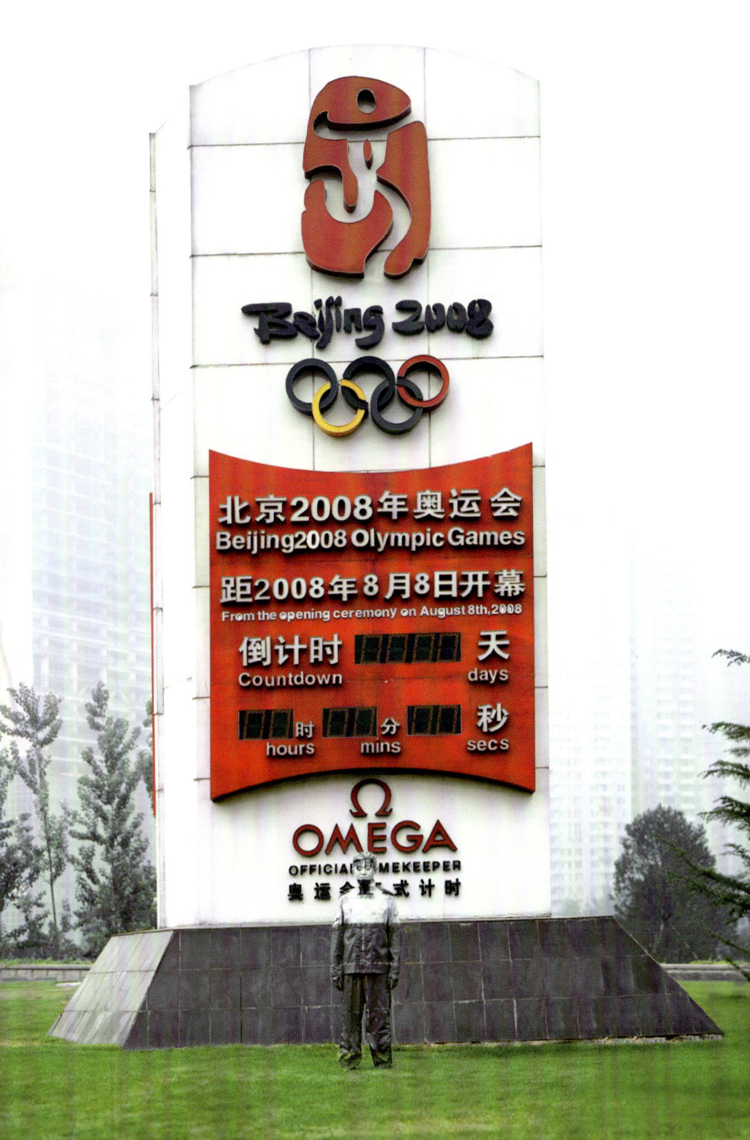
Beijing 2008
北京2008年奥运会
Beijing2008 Olympic Games
距2008年8月8日开幕
From the opening ceremony on August 8th,2008
倒计时
Countdown
天
days
时
hours
分
mins
秒
secs
OMEGA

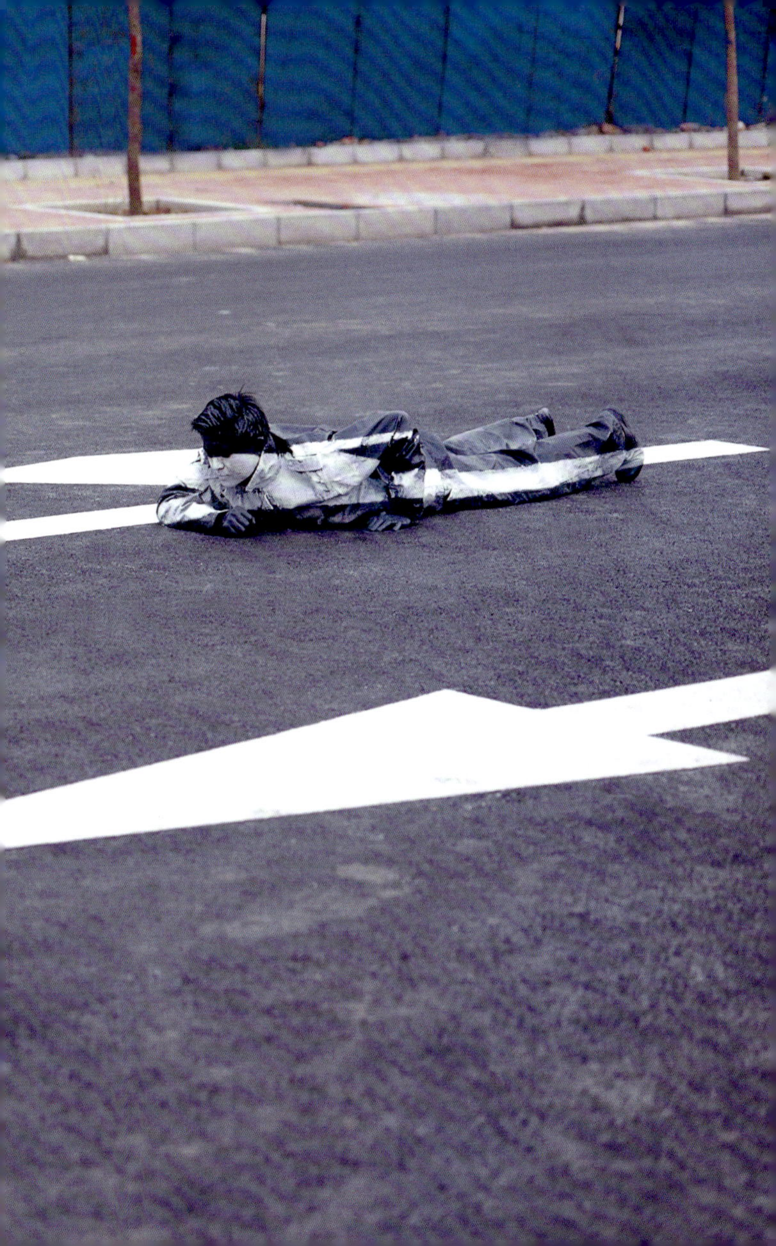

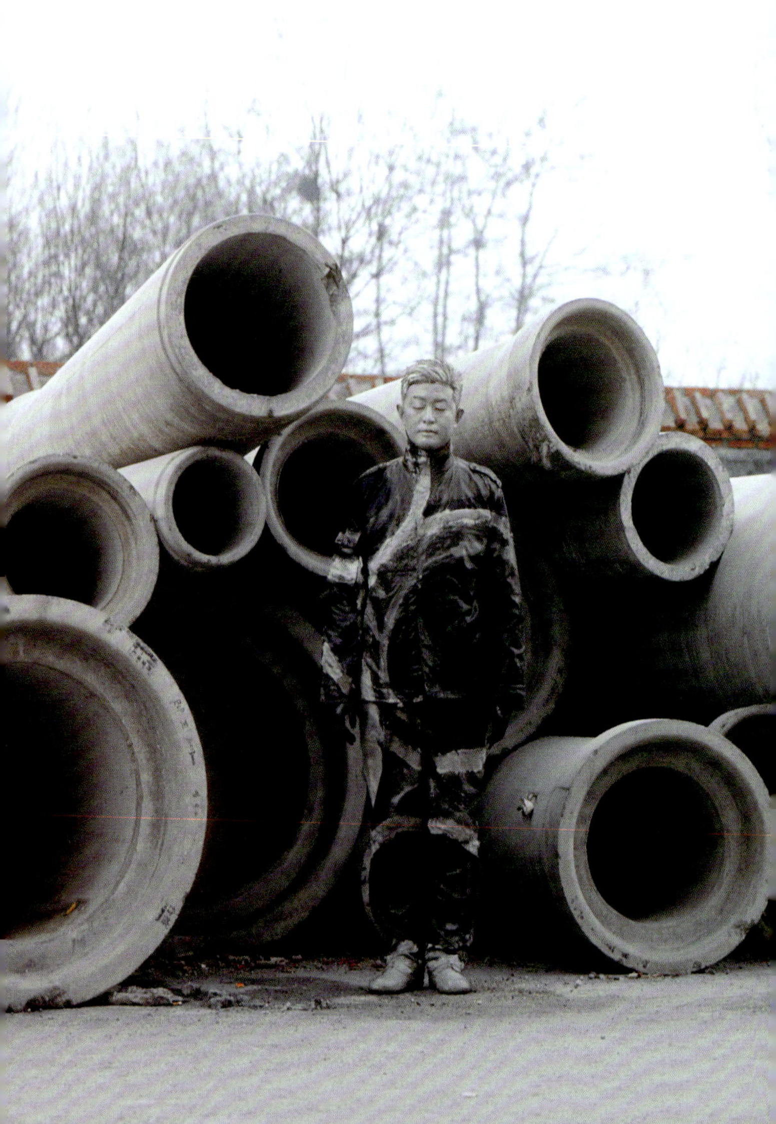

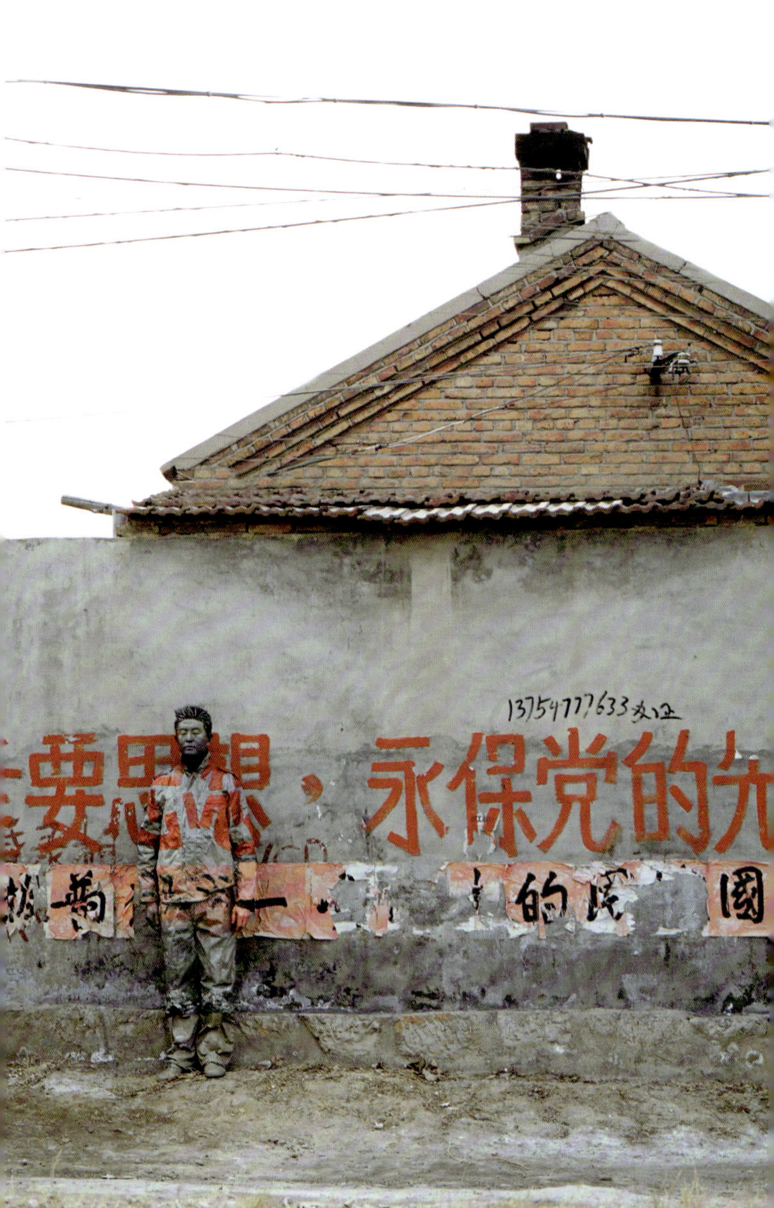

13754777633办证
永保党的

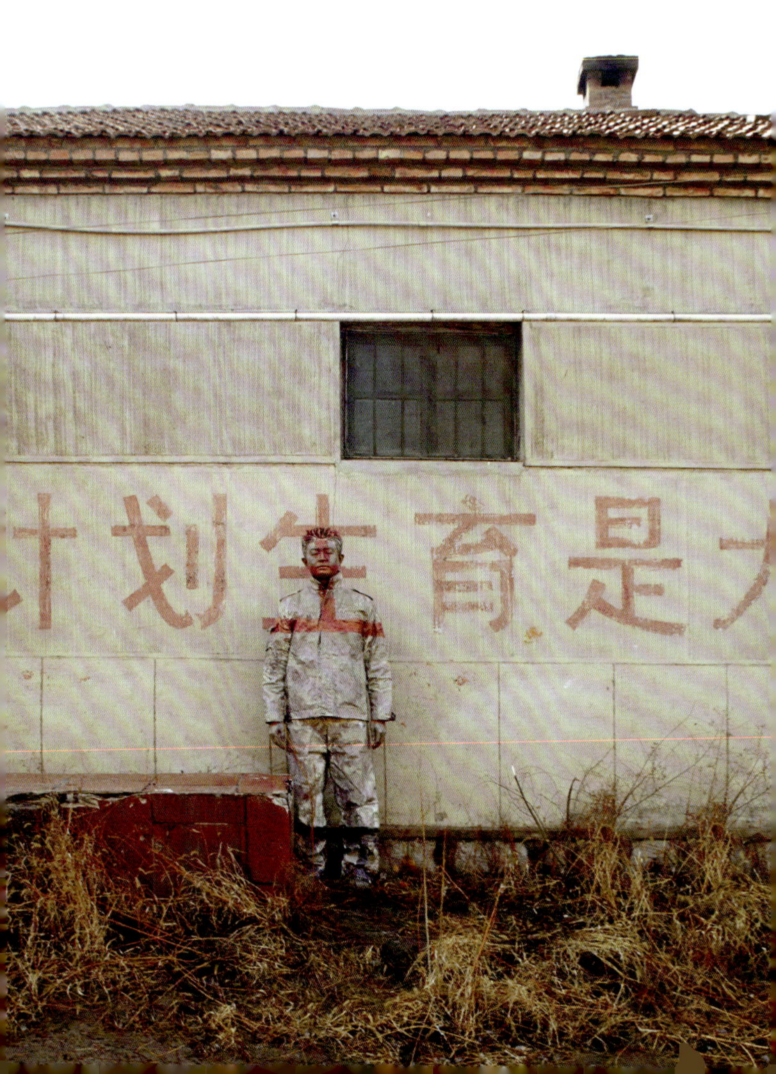
划生育是

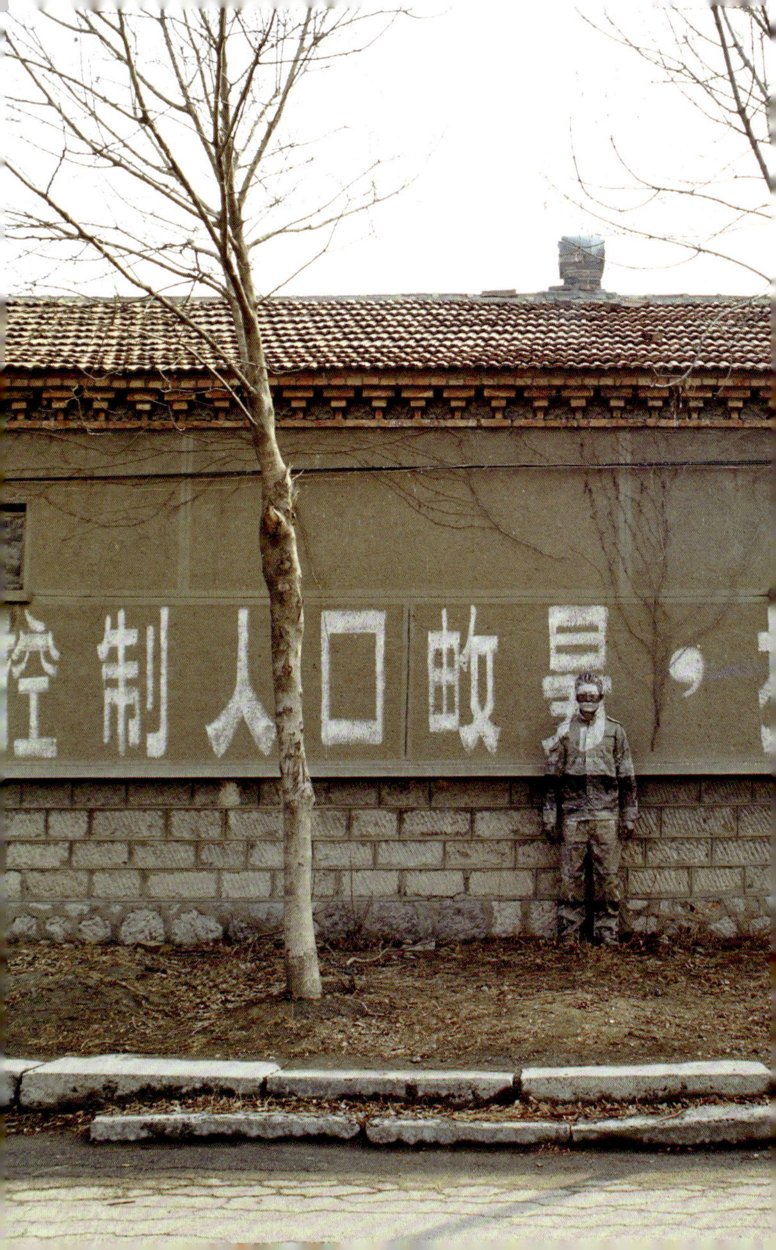
控制人口

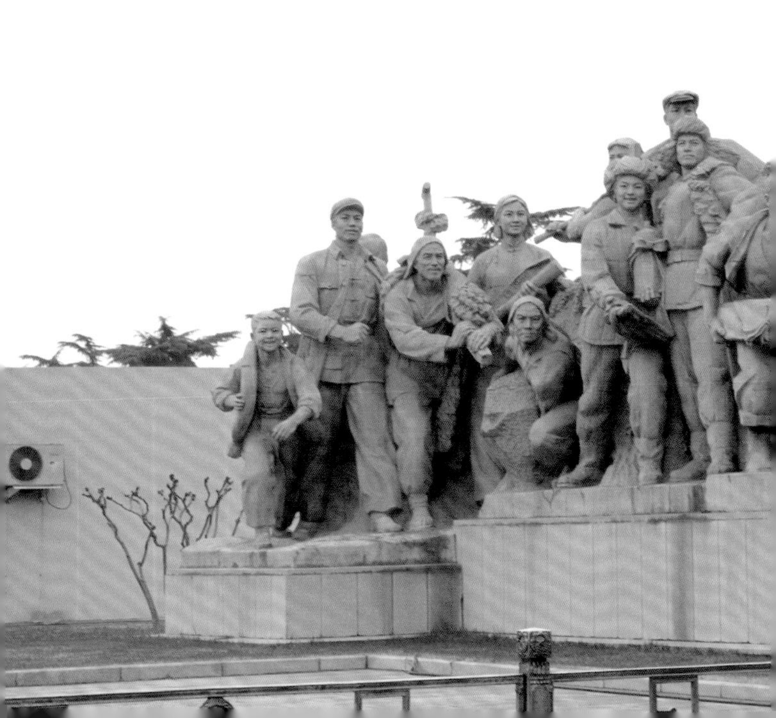

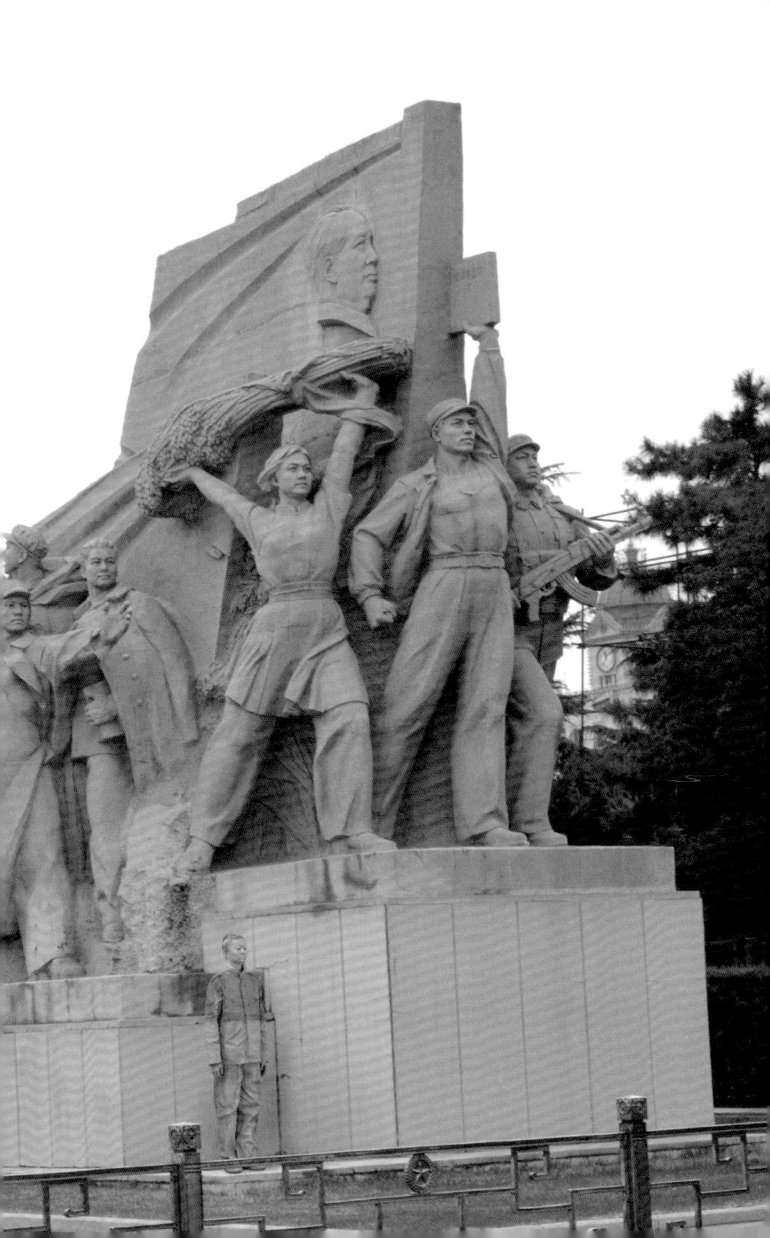

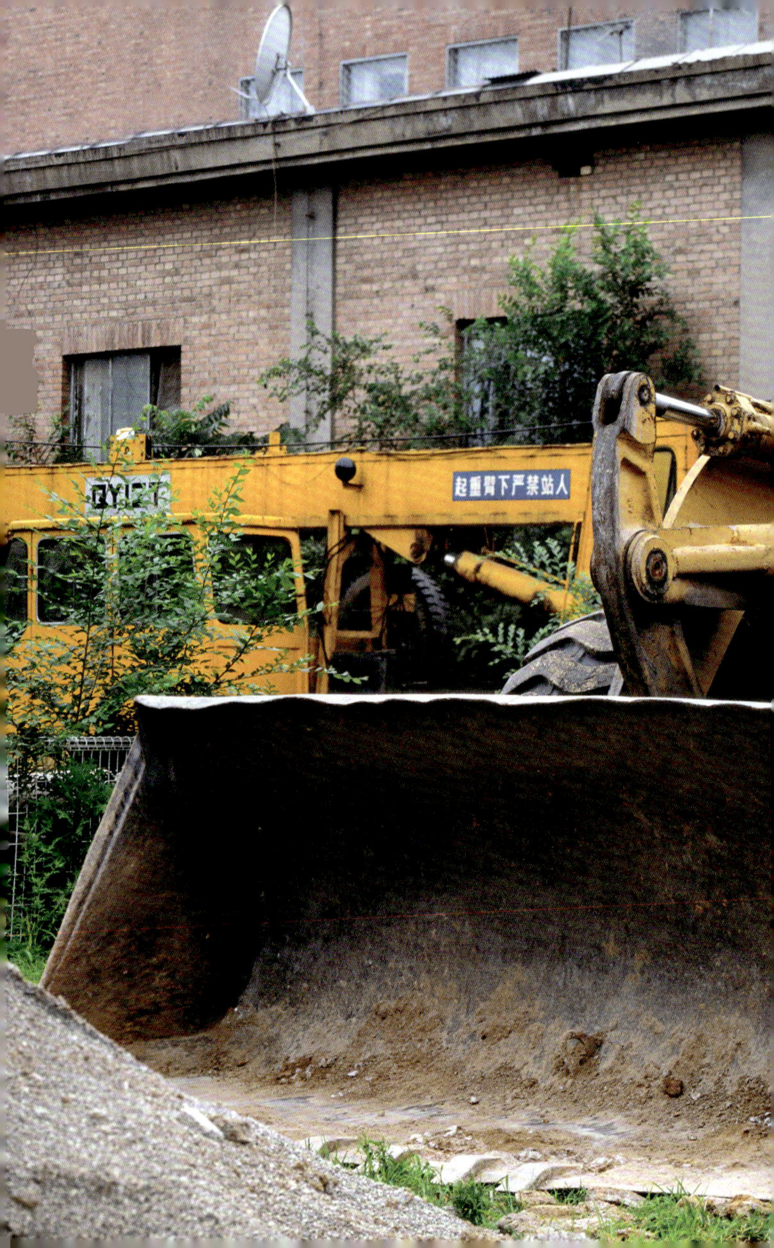
起重臂下严禁站人

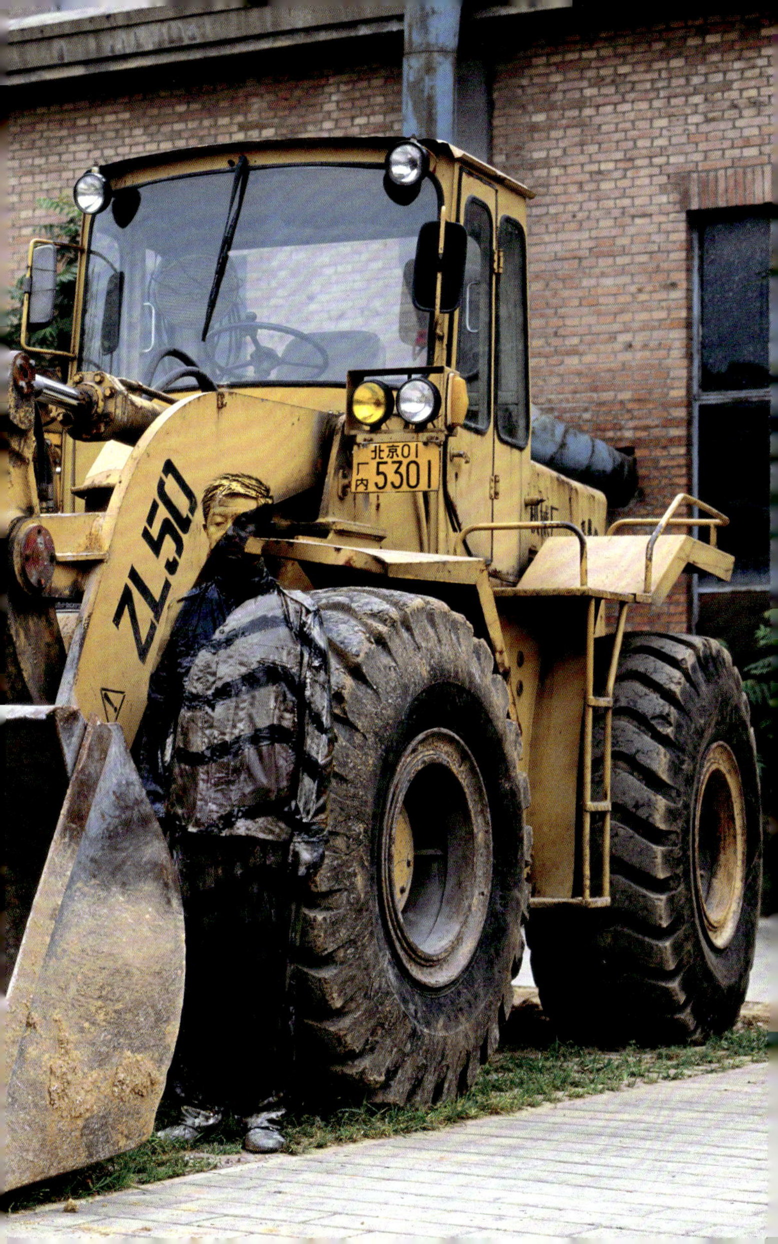
ZL50
北京01
厂内 5301

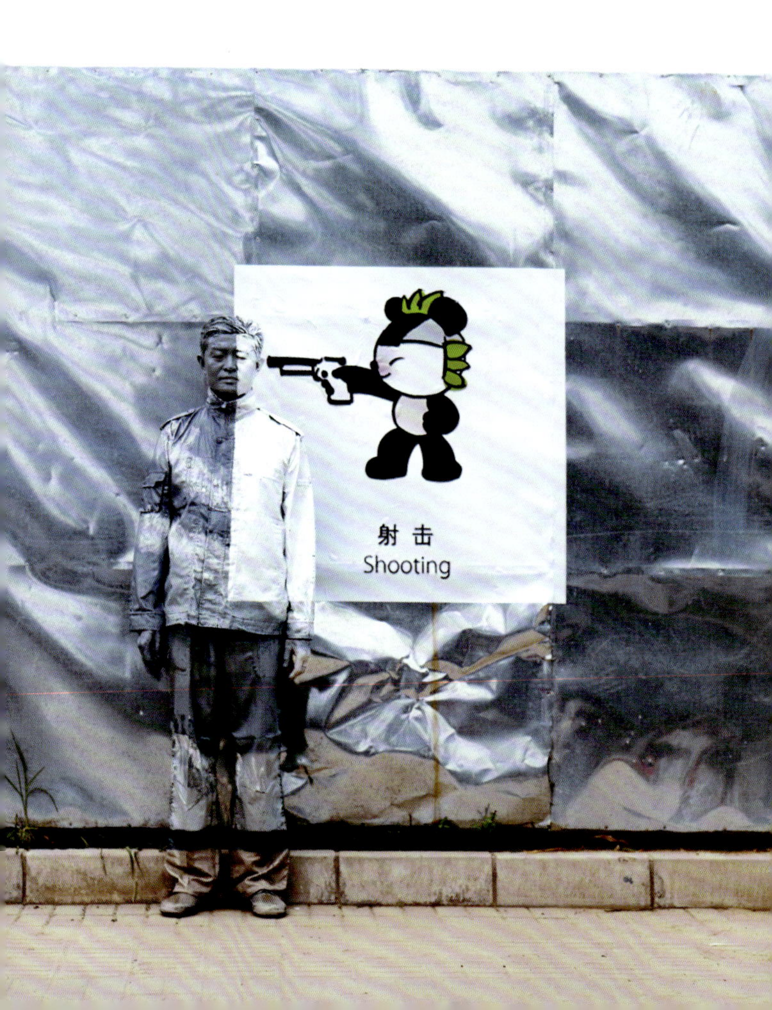
射 击
Shooting

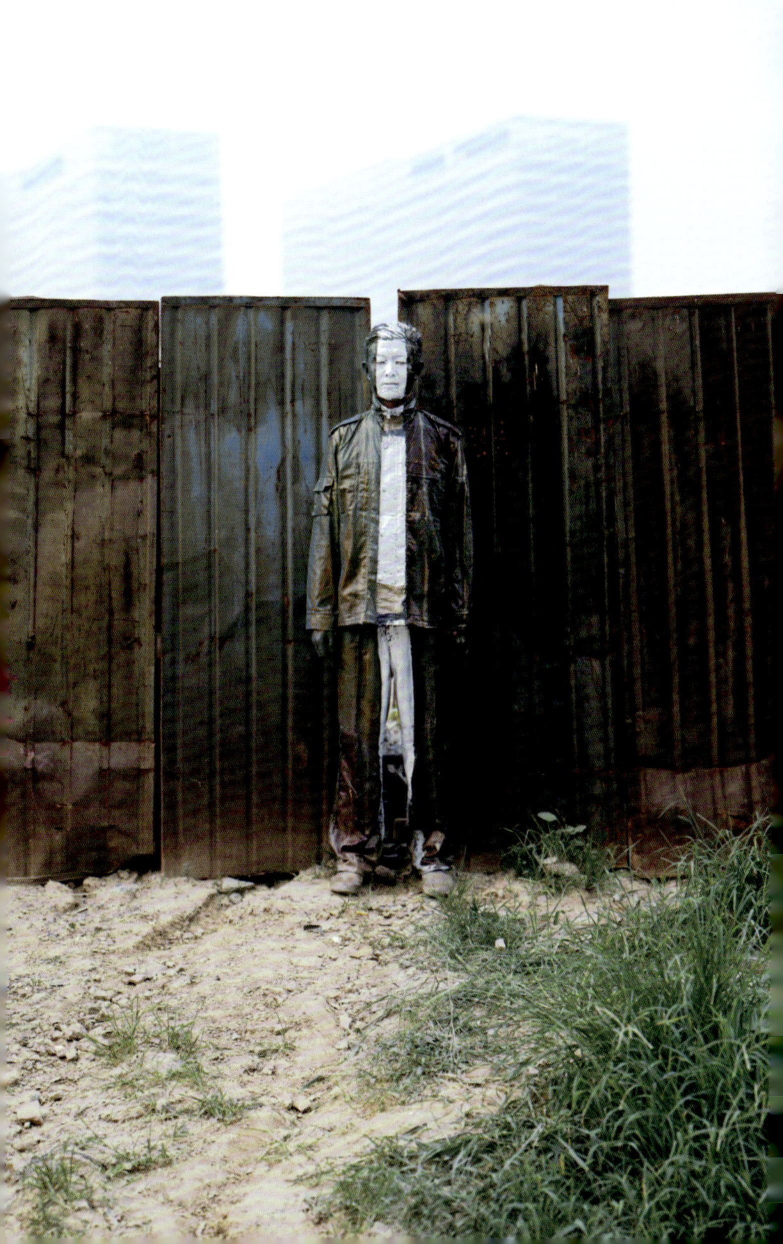

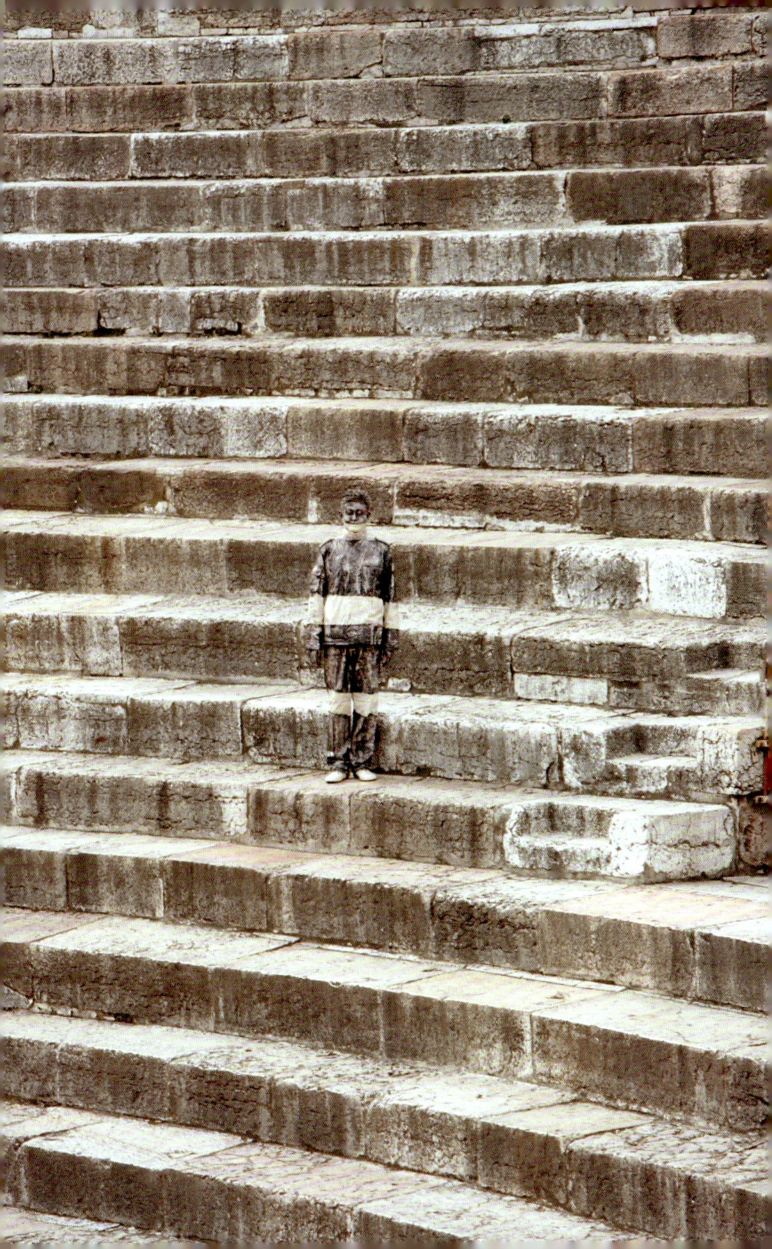

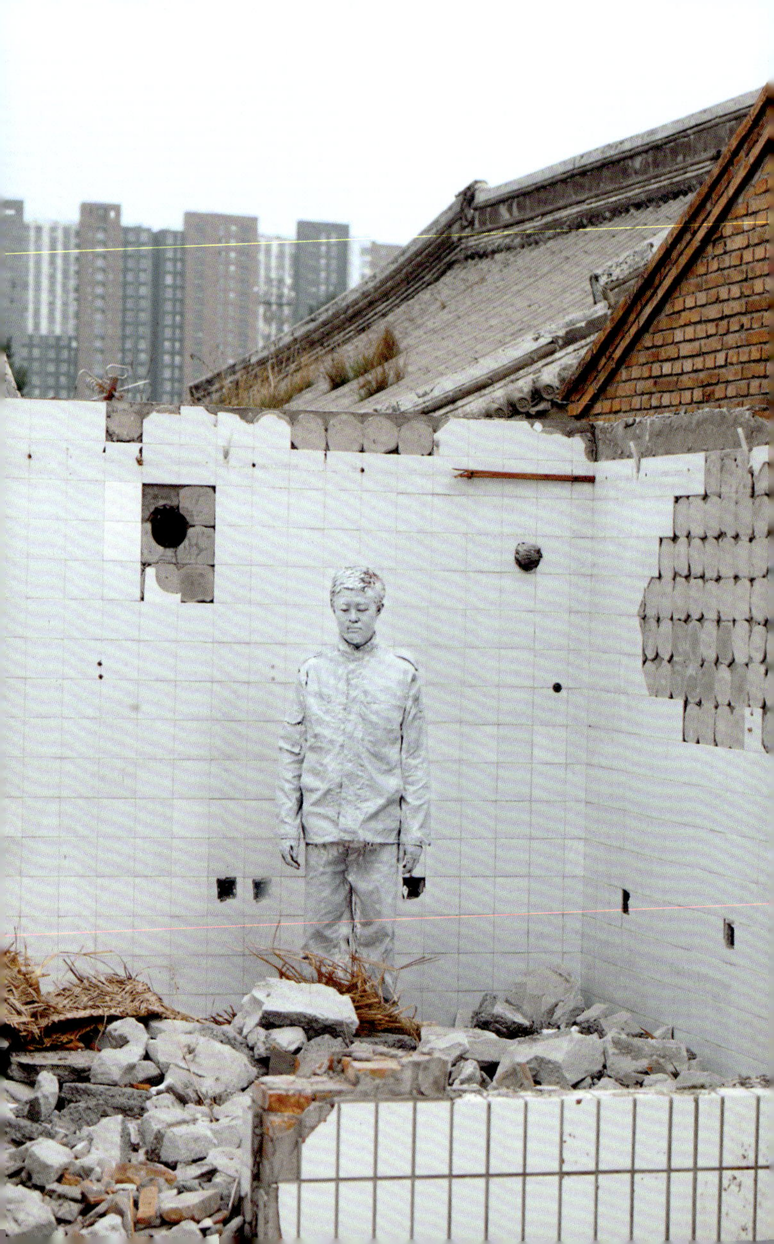

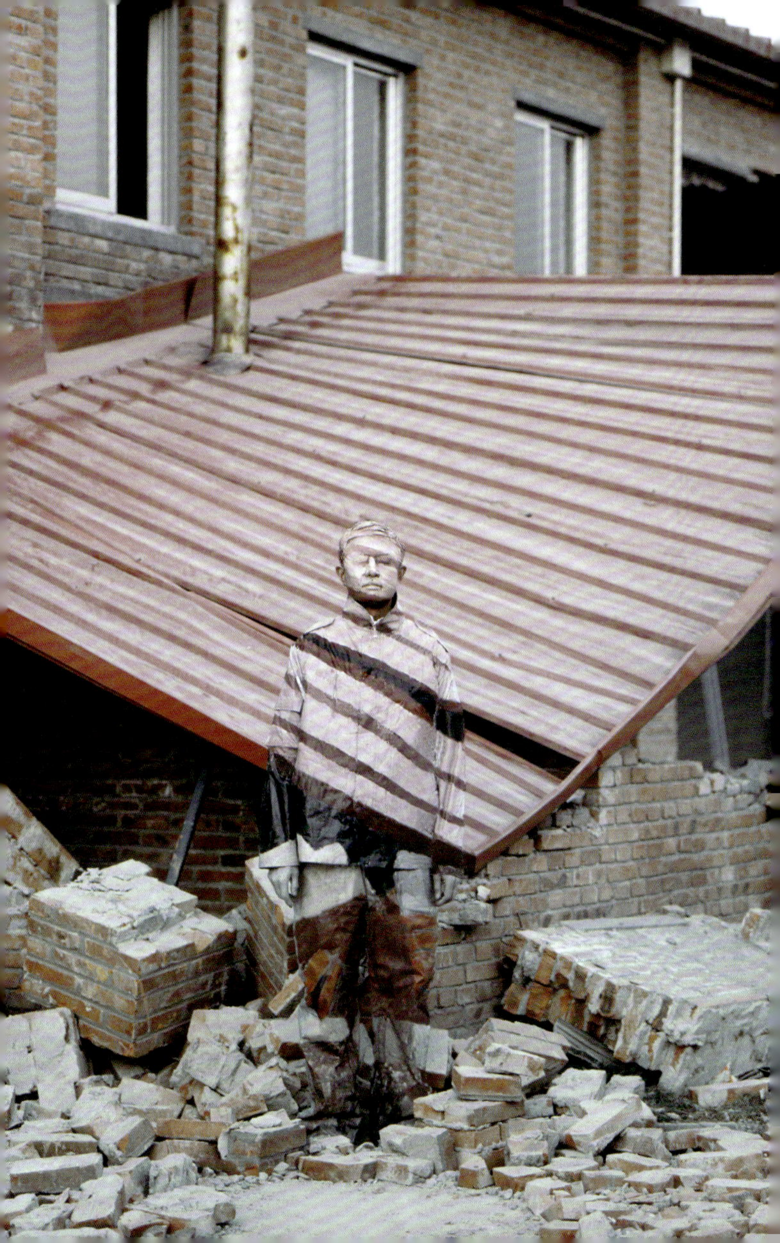

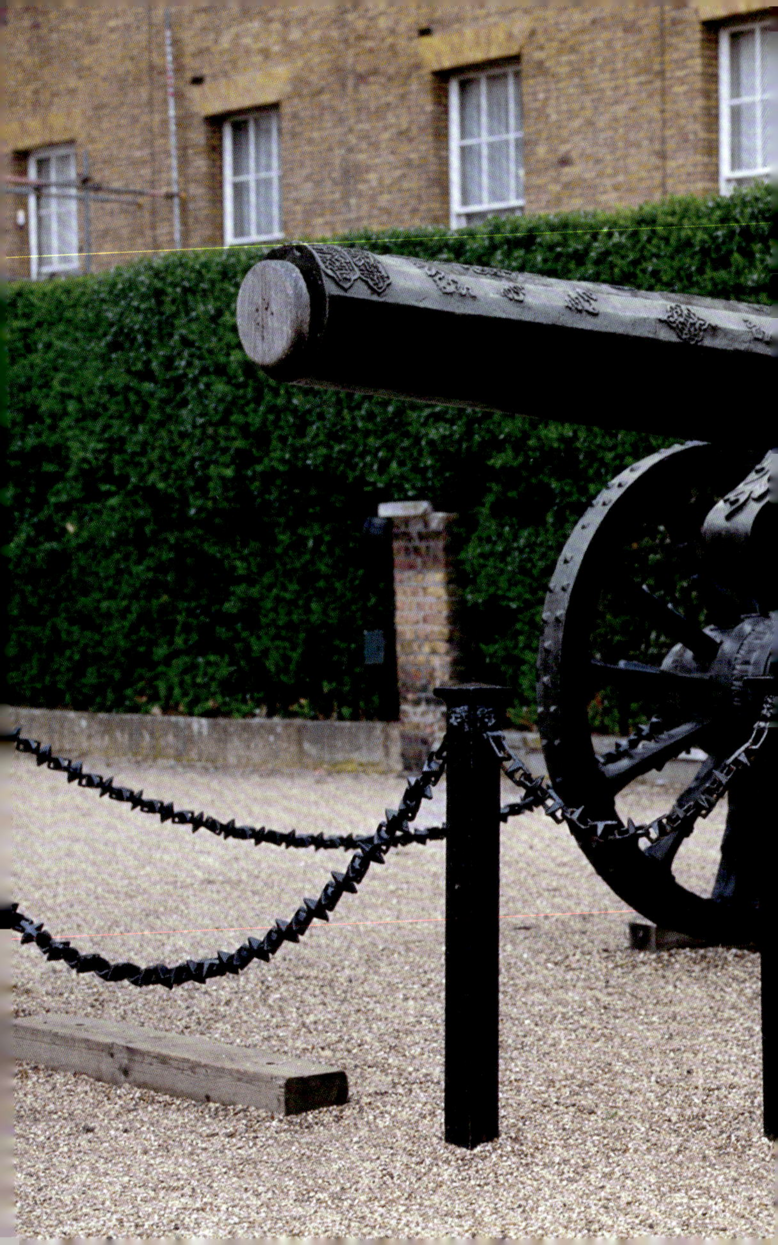

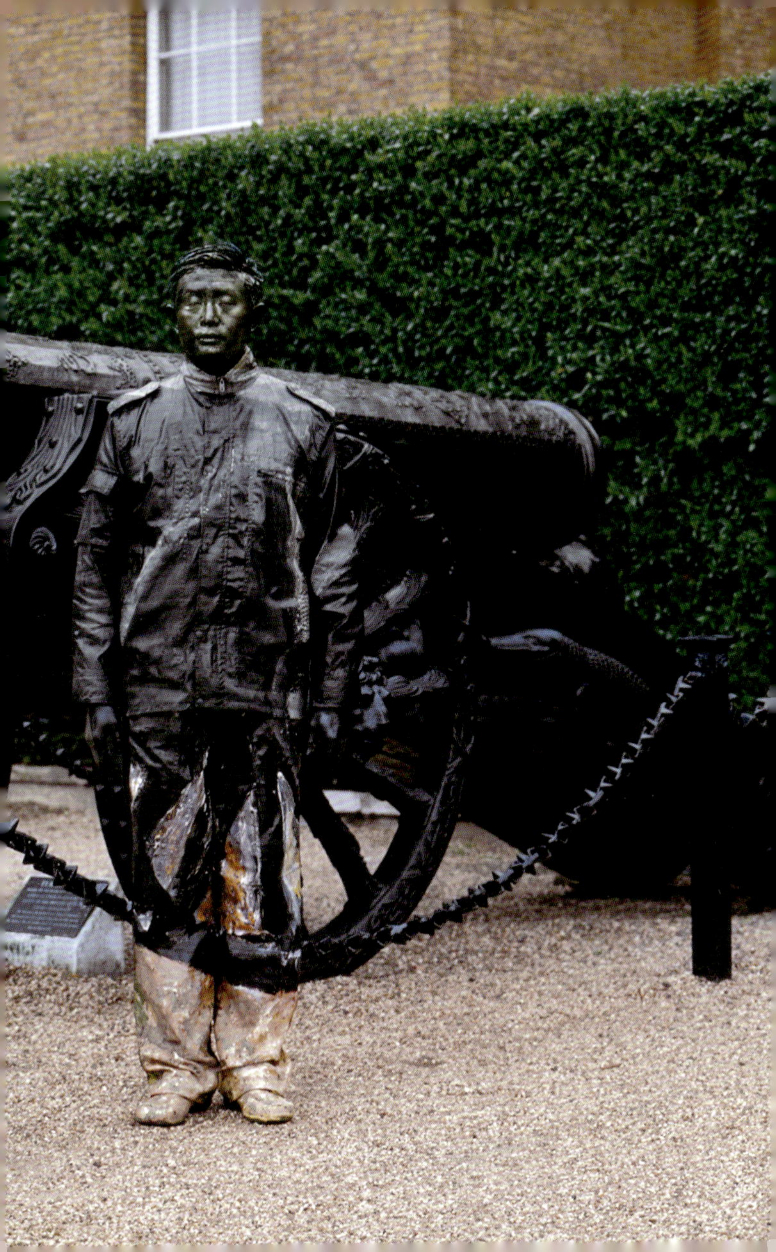

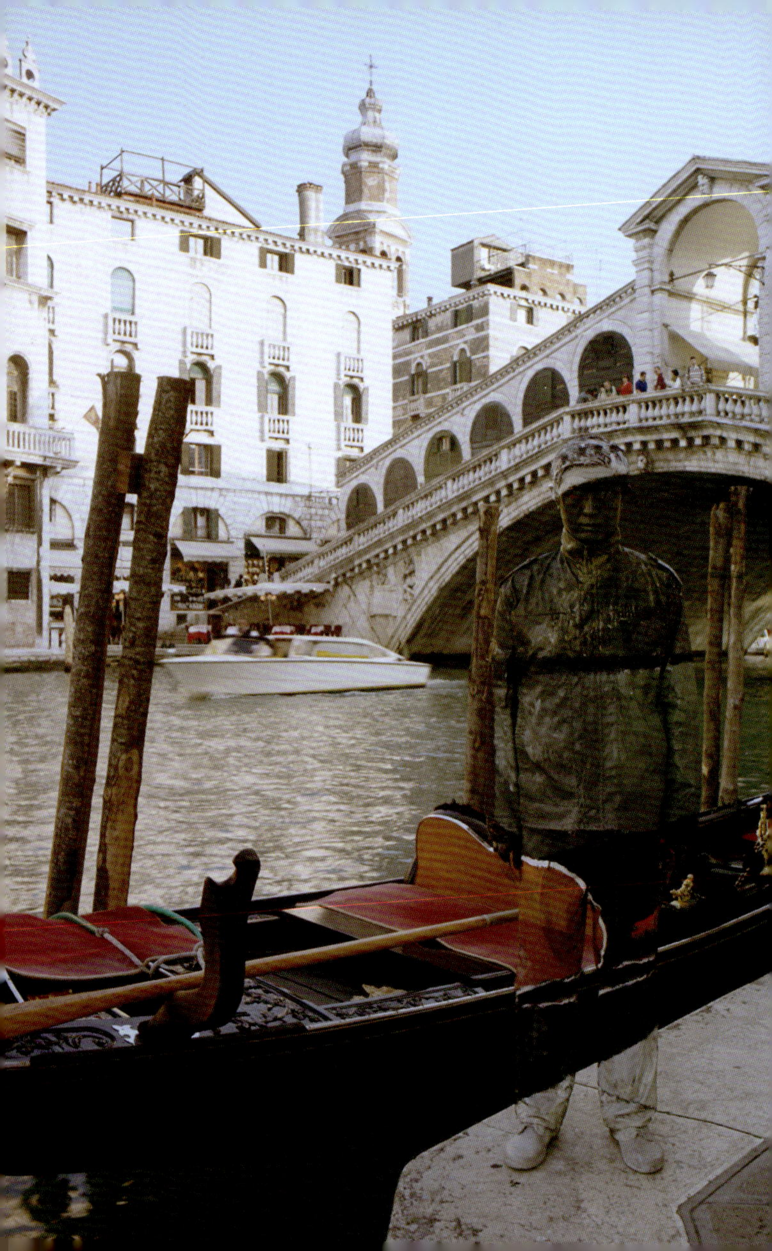

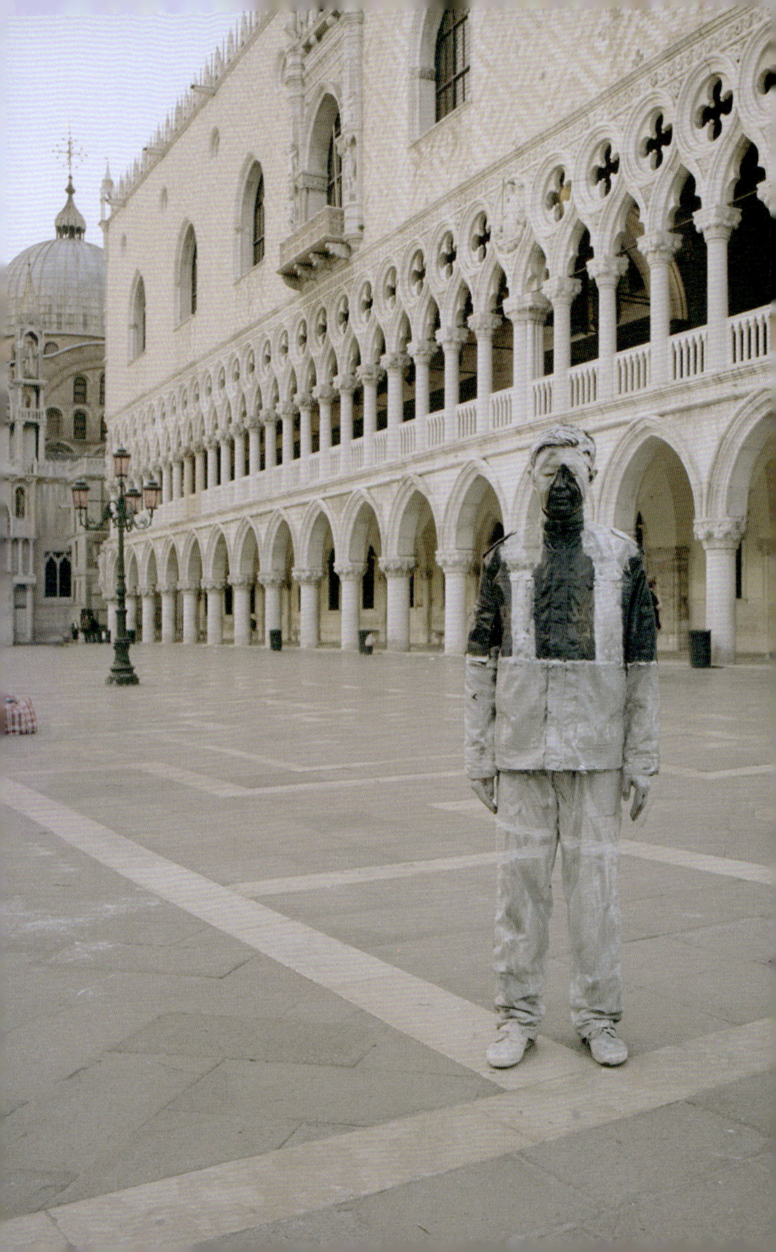

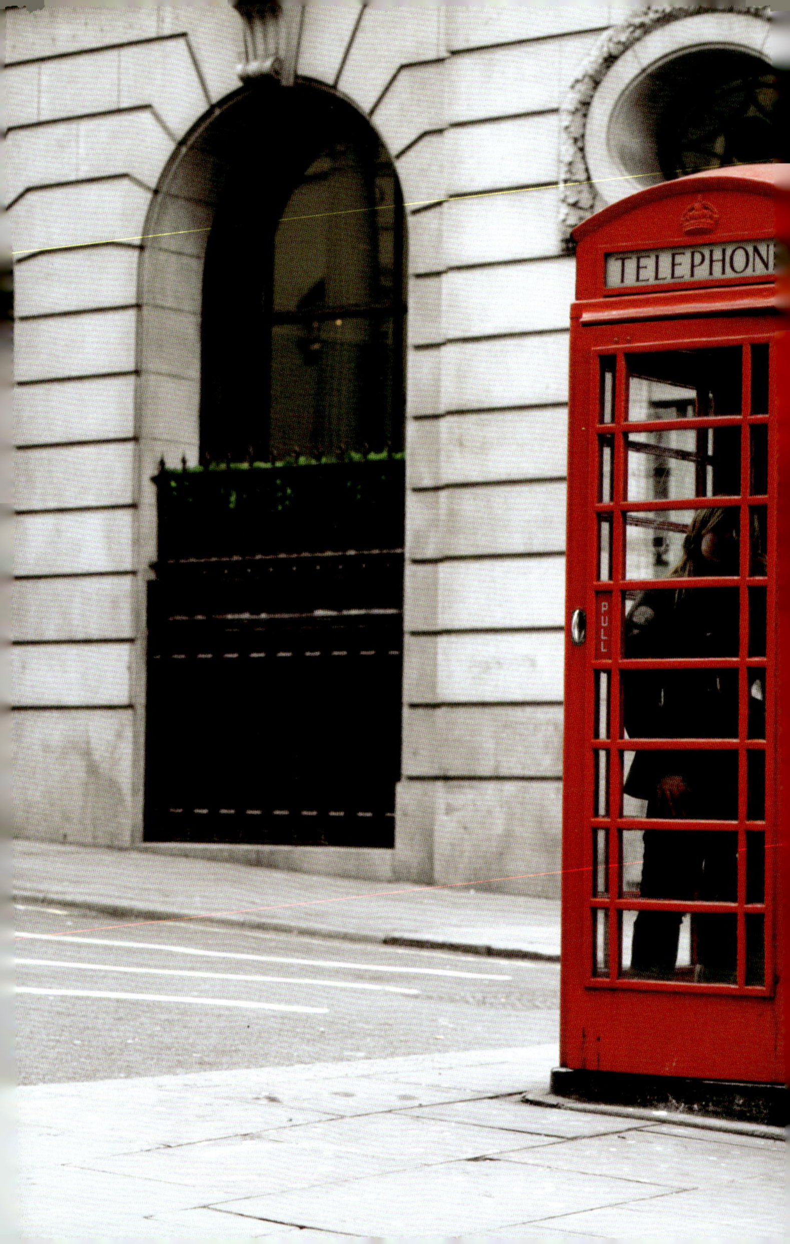
TELEPHON
PULL

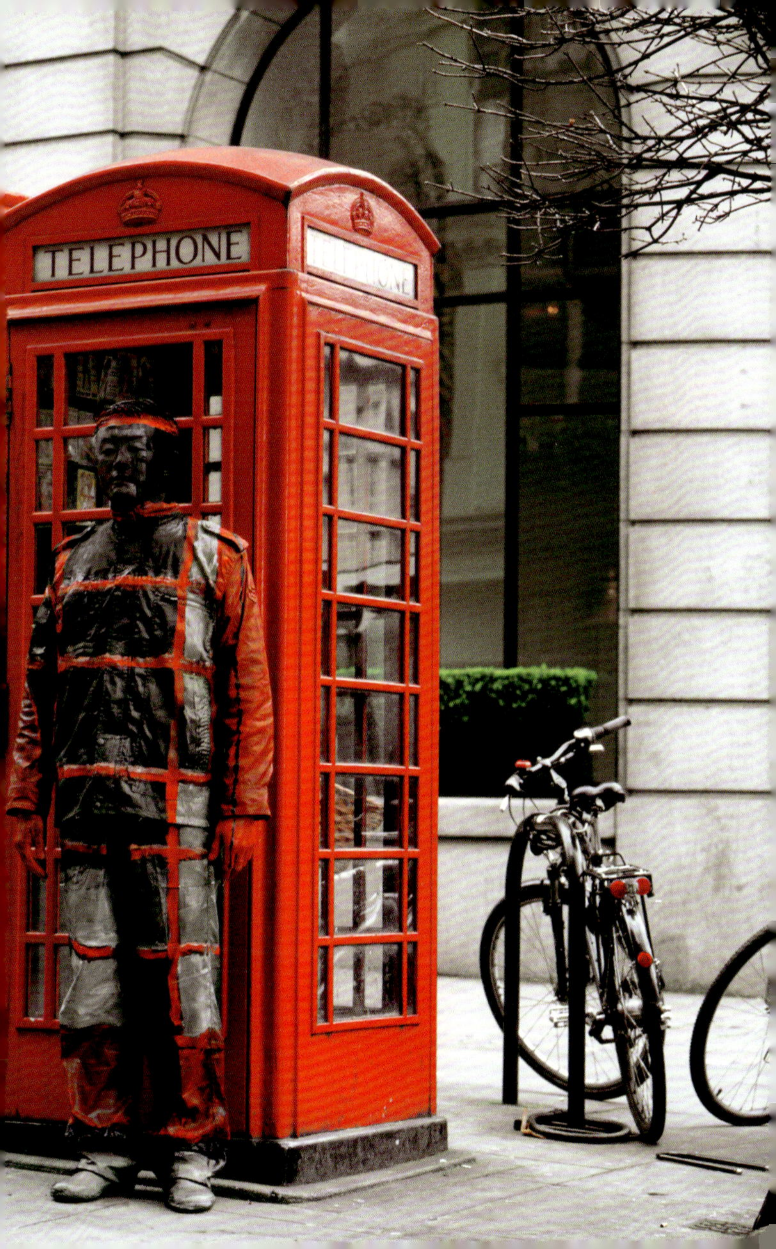
TELEPHONE

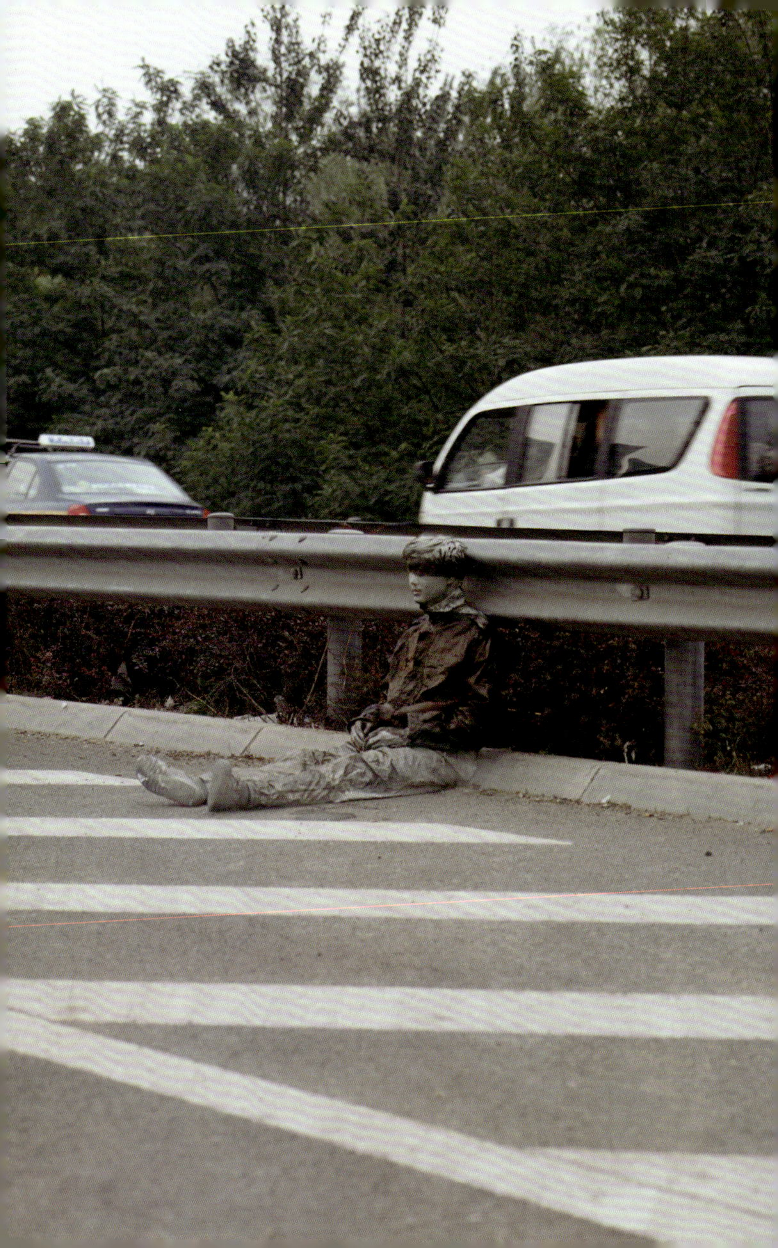

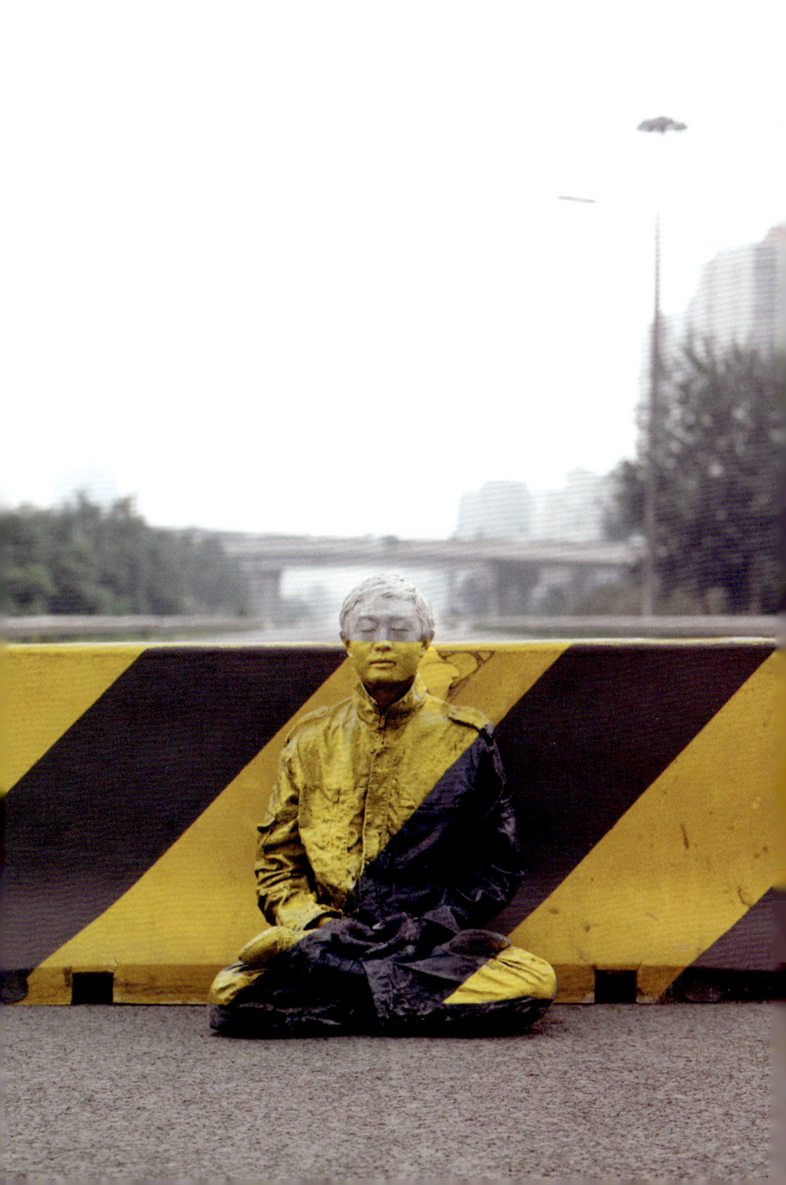

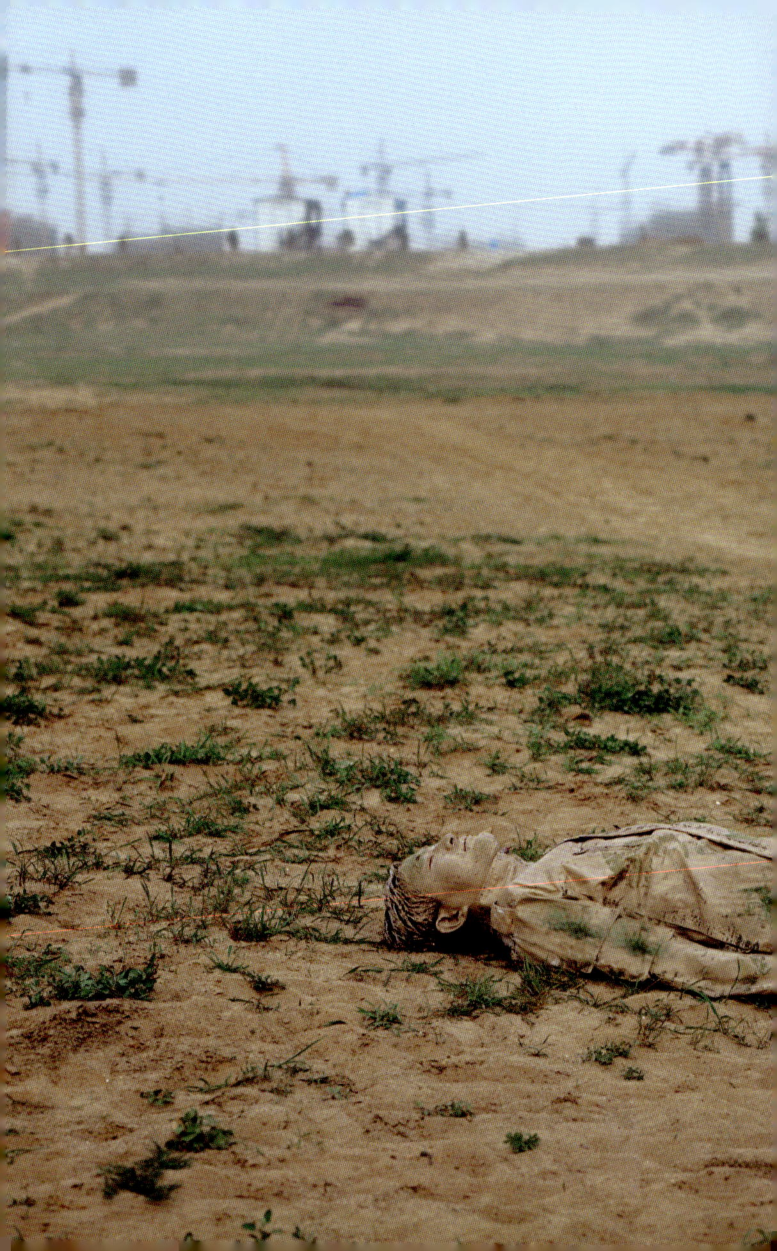

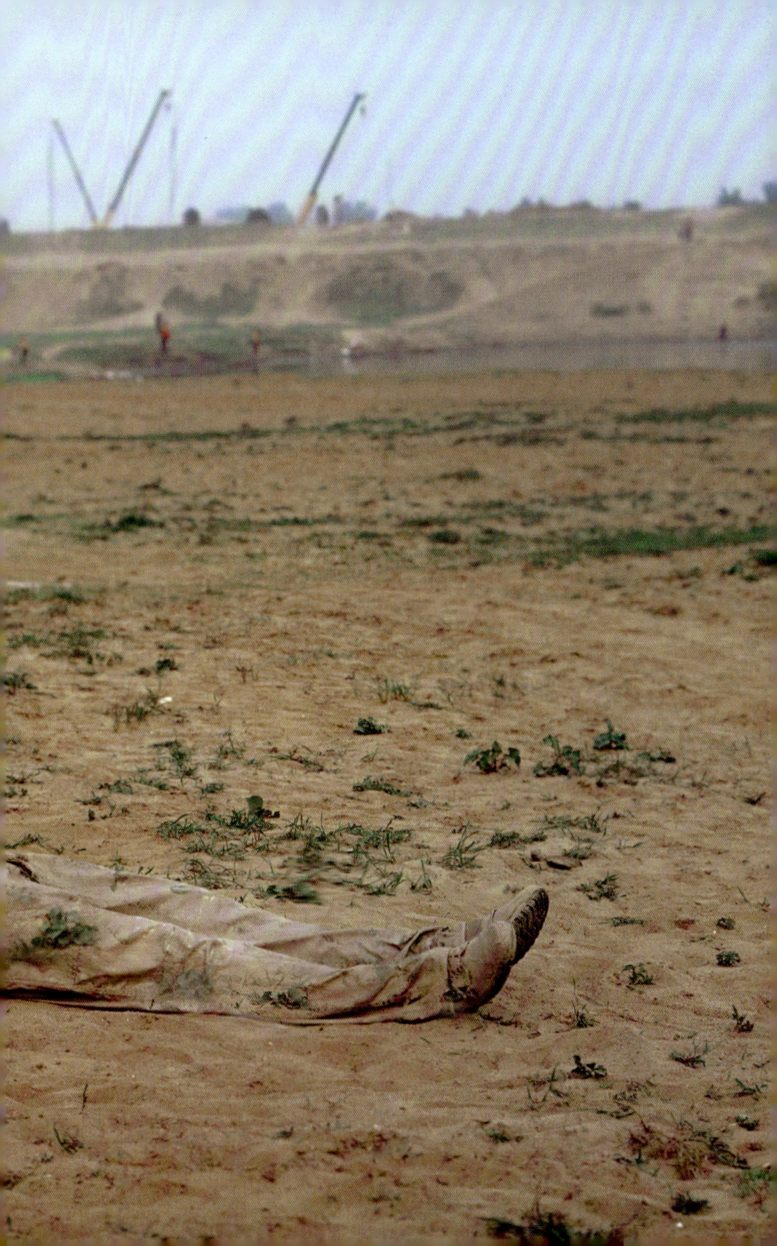

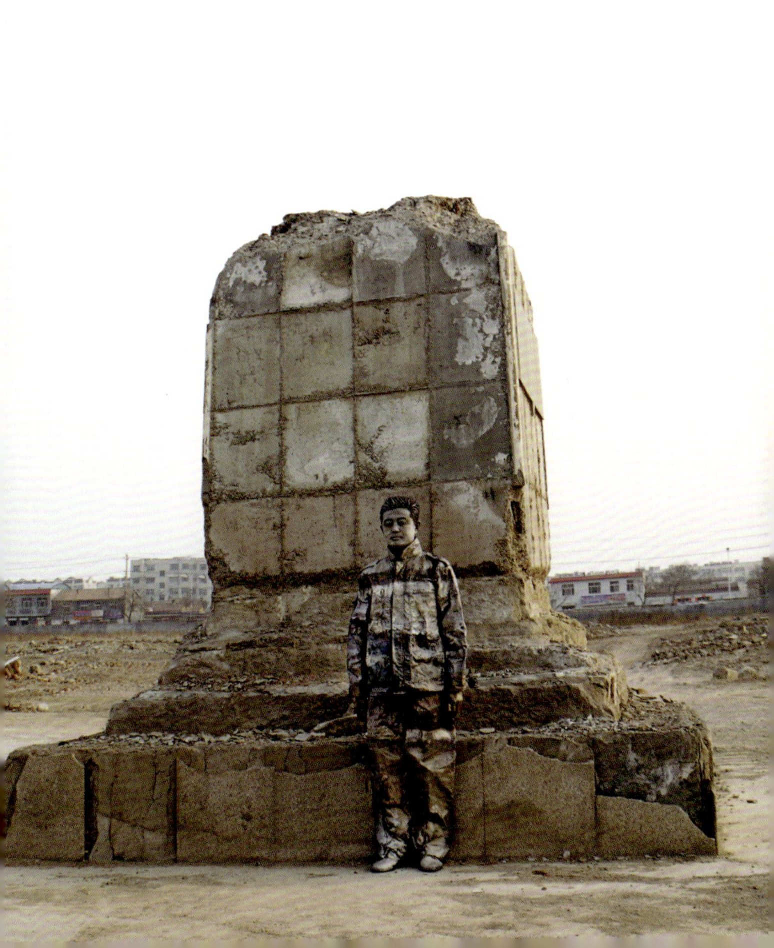

Index

1. Road Block - Oris **2.** Real Watches for Real People **3.** American Flag **4.** Pillars **5.** Temple of Heaven **6.** Pile of Bricks **7.** National Day **8.** Beijing New Art Project **9.** Erguo White Wine Factory **10.** Pile of Coal **11.** Face on a flag **12.** The Great Wall **13.** Monument **14.** New Culture Needs More **15.** Gray Opening Ceremony **16.** Open Field of Finance **17.** Voter's Registration is in Accordance with the Law **18.** La Scala Royal Box **19.** Monastery **20.** Supermarket II **21.** Greenbelt **22.** Unit 2 **23.** Graffiti I **24.** United Struggling **25.** La Scala **26.** Developing Socialism **27.** Arles **28.** Supermarket **29.** Construct an Harmonious Society Together **30.** Sawmill, Hiding in the City **31**. CCTV 1 **32.** CCTV 2 **33.** Olympic Emblem **34.** Beijing Welcomes You **35.** Nine Dragons Screen **36.** Graffiti II **37.** Construct an Harmonious Society Together **38.** Olympic Emblem **39.** Demolition **40.** Unify the Thought to Promote Education **41.** Hiding in the City **42.** Whole Family 2, Hiding in the City **43.** Nine Dragons Screen **44.** Hiding in the City **45.** August 9th **46.** Creeping Forward **47.** Pipes **48.** Keep the Advancement of the Party **49.** Family plan is the most important **50.** Contain the amount of the population, raise the quality of the population **51.** Sculptures on the Right of Chairman Mao's memorial **52.** Forklifts **53.** Shooting **54.** Rialto **55.** Piazza San Marco **56.** Telephone Booth **57.** Road **58.** Road Block **59.** Ancient Watercourse **60.** Ruins **61.** New Culture Needs More **62.** Bridge

This book is Published by
Ce livre est Publié par

Thircuir Limited.

Editor
Editeur

Enoia Ballade

Essay
Texte

Geneviève Brisac

Translation
Traduction

Thomas Bartz

Printed in China / Imprimé en Chine. info@thircuir.com www.thircuir.com